"MODERNISM" IN MODERN DRAMA

A Definition and an Estimate

"Modernism" in Modern Drama

A Definition and an Estimate

JOSEPH WOOD KRUTCH

NEW YORK

RUSSELL & RUSSELL · INC

COPYRIGHT 1953 BY CORNELL UNIVERSITY
PUBLISHED 1962 BY RUSSELL & RUSSELL, INC.
BY ARRANGEMENT WITH THE AUTHOR
L. C. CATALOG CARD NO: 62—10231

PRINTED IN THE UNITED STATES OF AMERICA

To Marjorie Nicolson

/ Foreword

ALL AGES are changing ages, but during the second half of the nineteenth century many people were convinced that theirs was such in a very special sense. They both believed and hoped that they were making a very radical break with the past, and they looked forward to a future really discontinuous with it. Some of them spoke of "tradition" as almost wholly bad. Something, they thought, was at last setting men free, and they tended to think of only two epochs in man's history, the Past and that Future of which they were seeing the dawn.

The term "modernism" is so vague and so general that no two people are likely to use it in the same way, and it ought not to be used at all unless this fact is taken for granted. I use it, not on the assumption that anyone will automatically know what I mean, but simply as a convenient way of making frequent reference to the special meaning which I have tried to give it. That special meaning includes, first, the tendency to believe that "modern" ideas are radically different from any generally entertained before and, second, certain more specific beliefs, doubts, attitudes, and judgments which seem to me characteristic of people who believed themselves to be "modernists" in the first sense just given. The thesis I have tried to develop is that the modern drama of Europe and America, like modern literature in general, affords much material from the examination of which may be obtained a clear idea of what some of the radically new, or at least supposedly new, ideas were. The conclusion drawn is that at least certain of these ideas are such that they inevitably lead, not to a bright future, but to something like intellectual and moral paralysis.

No one, I hope, will accuse me of being biased or unfair. Or rather I hope that no one will fail to understand that in order to make a point which I believe to be worth making I have permitted myself to be both biased and unfair—at least in so far as any presentation of only one side of a case is inevitably "unfair." In the essays that follow, more than once I disclaim any attempt to discuss the drama as such or to pass a literary judgment upon it. I speak as a moralist, not as a critic. Perhaps, however, it is well to go even further and to admit that my purpose is frankly polemic. I had and I have an ax to grind. I seek to persuade my readers that much of what others have presented to them as the convictions necessary to anyone who wished to believe himself "modern" is actually incompatible with any good life as the good life has generally been conceived of during many centuries before the nineteenth. In defense of my method I might cite the opinion of a good modernist, Bernard Shaw, who once maintained that the best way to get at the truth of a matter is not to try to be impartial but to have it debated with reckless partiality from both sides. It is something like this which I from my side attempt to do.

Except for minor changes and the inclusion of a few paragraphs omitted because of lack of time, this printed text is what my audience heard when I delivered at Cornell University in October, 1952, the series of Messenger Lectures entitled "'Modernism' in Modern Drama: A Definition and an Estimate." Had I been writing a book to be read I should no doubt have written it somewhat differently. Things must be stated downrightly and without too much caution or qualification if they are to be caught on the wing. But the reader of what purports to be lectures has a right, I think, to read lectures rather than the second thoughts of the lecturer.

J. W. K.

/ Contents

"MODERNISM" IN MODERN DRAMA

A Definition and an Estimate

1 / Ibsen and the Chasm between Past and Future

IN MODERN times the current acted drama has generally been regarded as a minor department of literature. Since it was reborn in the Middle Ages, it has usually been written to fill the needs of a theater, and since the days of Shakespeare the theater in England and America has been predominantly a commercial institution devoted primarily to the business of supplying a popular entertainment.

For that reason, if for no other, students of literature have been disinclined to take its current manifestations very seriously. This was true in Shakespeare's time, when few educated men would have supposed it possible that the Elizabethan drama would one day be considered the chief glory of Elizabethan literature. It is equally true today when the most earnest literary critics seldom devote their attention to any modern dramatist.

1

Eugene O'Neill received the Nobel Prize, but his admirers are to be found most often among those especially interested in the theater and perhaps among members of the general public—rarely among critics of belles-lettres. Shaw and Chekhov have, perhaps, been admitted into the canon, but neither holds a very high place and both are less likely to be discussed in, let us say, the more pretentious quarterlies than Lorca or Cocteau or T. S. Eliot, whose plays have won no wide acceptance in the popular theater.

With the rightness or wrongness of this attitude I have at the moment little concern. The subject at hand is not the greatness or the defects of the modern drama considered as a contribution to world literature. Instead I intend to use modern drama chiefly as a body of evidence from which I think certain conclusions can be drawn concerning the development of ideas that have affected and continue to affect most of us very profoundly.

I have no doubt that many of my conclusions could be drawn equally well—some would say much better—either from imaginative literature in other forms or from writings of the philosophers, the scientists, and the sociologists contemporary with these dramatists. But I have two reasons for choosing, somewhat perversely perhaps, to look for them in the drama instead.

Perhaps the more important of these reasons is simply that I happen to have been professionally concerned with the drama for more than a quarter of a century and am more familiar with it than I am with any other body of modern literature. The second reason is that if we are looking, as I am, for ideas and attitudes characteristic and widespread there may be a certain advantage in choosing material which was intended for a wide public.

The poet and the philosopher sometimes operate in a semiprivate world. They have no general audience in mind; they may intend to speak only to a very limited group. Even the dissident and revolutionary dramatist, however, knows that if he is writing for the theater rather than for the closet he must at least aim to reach masses of people. He must think of what he has to say as at least potentially popular. He must hope to win for his attitudes some sort of general acceptance. If Bernard Shaw, for example, borrows from Nietzsche and Bergson and if his plays ultimately reach a wide audience, that is evidence that these ideas really were acceptable to the audience for which he wrote. For that reason, if one wants to draw conclusions concerning the spirit of the age, it is safer to cite Shaw than it is to cite philosophers who might, however brilliant, have affected chiefly other philosophers. We might speculate concerning the extent to which these philosophers really influenced the mental attitudes of the society in which they lived. On the other hand, we know that some general public found Shaw congenial.

We shall not have to go very far back in our search for evidence. During a considerable part of the eighteenth and nineteenth centuries the contemporary acted drama in England and America was both intellectually and artistically stagnant. From, shall we say, the death of Sheridan to the emergence of Oscar Wilde, no Englishman and no American of considerable talent devoted himself chiefly to writing plays. The theater, though it was sometimes commercially flourishing, was generally considered as nonliterary and as intellectually dead as it was artistically null.

Instead of laboring this point, it will be sufficient to cite a jibe in one of Shaw's early plays which sums up the situation rather well. In *You Never Can Tell*, a Victorian "ad-

vanced thinker" returns from long residence abroad to discover that her shocking ideas about woman's rights, political
democracy, and the like are no longer shocking. It is gently
explained to her that only one British institution still operates
on the assumption that such ideas are advanced. "You
mean," she says, "the Church." "Oh no," replied the Shavian
expositor, "I mean the theater."

Shaw was, of course, speaking in the interests of the new
dramatists of whom the public was just beginning to be somewhat resentfully aware. A few years before *You Never Can
Tell* appeared, the first play by Henrik Ibsen had been performed in London, and that unexpected phenomenon which
we still call modern drama—despite the fact that it is by now
at least three-quarters of a century old—had been launched
in the English-speaking world.

For our purposes it is not necessary to inquire how it
happened that a literary form which had been all but given
up as an instrument of serious expression, either intellectual
or artistic, should have become, as for a time it certainly did,
perhaps the most important species of imaginative writing
so far as the dissemination of revolutionary attitudes is concerned. We shall simply accept the familiar fact that for the
first time in several generations the intellectually restless
began to see, or more often simply to read, dramatic works—
not usually because they had any special interest in the
theater but because to read them was the surest and simplest
way of doing what we call "keeping up with the times."
Ibsenism tended to become the key to modernism.

To repeat, my principal purpose is to describe and to try
to evaluate some of the convictions and the attitudes which
reached and are still reaching us through the drama. What
I am concerned with is the meaning of what was called in the

eighteen-nineties "modernism." By that I mean both the ideas themselves and the conviction, then and now so widespread, that to be "modern" is to be, in many important ways, different from any one who ever lived before.

Perhaps the best place to start is with two phrases from a letter which Henrik Ibsen wrote to Georg Brandes at a time when Ibsen, though already in his forties, had not yet written A Doll's House, which is conveniently taken as the first of his successful social plays.

Shortly before the letter was written Brandes had published his huge Main Currents in Nineteenth-Century Literature, of which the most obvious leading principle is the assumption that there is something in spirit and intention which can be called "modern" and that all writers of the recent past can be judged as well as classified by the degree to which their allegiance is given to "the modern" or the traditional.

In our own day we are at least as familiar with a reaction against this attitude as we are with the attitude itself. T. S. Eliot has again made familiar a stress upon continuity and tradition, even upon the conviction that it is necessary to make contact again with the past. Nowadays we are often more than dubious about "modernism." To some it seems more like a subtle disease than like an advance into freedom and light. But Brandes had faith in the future, and Ibsen found Brandes' concept more than congenial. He says in his letter that he could think of nothing else by day or night. "It is," he wrote, "one of those books which open a great chasm between yesterday and to-day." A little later, his excitement rising, he declares a "war to the knife between two epochs."

Ibsen had begun, it must be remembered, as a traditional

writer whose first plays had dealt with legends of the national past and who had spoken of the necessity for reviving the poetic spirit of olden days. For some time, however, he had been moving uncertainly and tentatively in the direction of realism and social problems, and Brandes' book seems to have produced a clarification, almost to have precipitated a conversion. Thereafter the concept of the past as the enemy of the future and of the present, the conviction that we must attempt some sort of difficult leap across the chasm which separated the two, became a dominant idea, almost an obsession. The villain of his dramas becomes the voices from the past, called ghosts in his most famous work and typified by "the Rosmer way" in another.

Since we ourselves, in the course of this discussion, are to be deeply concerned with this fateful concept of the future as somehow discontinuous with the past and since, for convenience' sake, we are taking Ibsen as our starting point, we should remind ourselves before continuing that so to take him is in part only a matter of convenience—that although, in the drama at least, Ibsen was the first fully effective exponent of the idea, he did not either invent it or even first introduce it into the drama.

Thus, for example, as early as 1844, when Ibsen was only sixteen years old and employed as a pharmacist's assistant in a Norwegian village, the German dramatist Friedrich Hebbel had written a play called *Maria Magdalena*. Hebbel had previously been known chiefly for historical tragedies, but *Maria Magdalena* is, despite its title, a curious anticipation of Ibsen both in its subject matter and in its suggestion of the revolutionary character of the supposed difference between the old and the new.

The hero of *Maria Magdalena* is a carpenter, poor but

honest and rigidly conventional. His pride in his working-man's respectability is dealt a cruel blow when his son is unjustly accused of theft. Final destruction comes when his daughter confesses that she is about to give birth to a child by a fiancé who has deserted her. The father is overwhelmed by the sense of impending disgrace. The daughter confesses that she cannot really feel the sense of terrible sin which her father thinks that she should. In the end he kills himself, not so much because of the disgrace itself, as because of what seems to him his daughter's wicked refusal to acknowledge her transgression. His last words are, "I do not understand the world anymore," and they have a curious Ibsenian ring. The important thing in Hebbel's play is not the realistic treatment of a contemporary situation or even the implied criticism of the current sexual morality. The important thing is the sense of a discontinuity between the worlds in which the father and the daughter live, of the impossibility of communication across the chasm which separates the past from the future.

Though Hebbel was by no means unknown he did not, however, go forth like Ibsen to conquer the world. We are therefore justified in taking Ibsen as our starting point.

Since our purpose is to trace, through the work of some of the leading modern dramatists, the meaning, the implications, and the consequences of this conviction that a radical break was being made with the past and since each important dramatist made an individual contribution or placed somewhat differently his emphasis, we shall have to consider what each seemed to mean by his explicit or implied acceptance of the general thesis. I should perhaps warn you that, in the beginning, at least, and simply for the sake of convenient exposition, we shall have to accept the dramatists' own point of view more completely than we shall later perhaps want to do.

To a certain degree we are by now living in what was to them "the future." In some respects the chasm seems wider and deeper than it seemed to them, the revolution more complete than they anticipated. Sometimes we may even wonder if we have not rather fallen into the gulf than crossed it. But such considerations as these belong to a later part of our discussion, and for the present we are concerned with what Hebbel as well as Ibsen had in mind. Why could old people not understand the world any longer; what was the gulf between the past and the future?

In the case of no other major modern dramatist are those questions quite so hard to answer as in the case of Ibsen himself. Increasingly he took the attitude, or assumed the pose, of a veiled prophet. He refused resolutely to explain his own plays or to commit himself on public questions. He joined no parties, took no part in movements, and insisted that he was a man who wrote plays, not a man who set earnest seekers right. His business, he once stated, was to ask questions, not to answer them, and in a speech made somewhat late in life he said, "I have been more of a poet and less of a social philosopher than is commonly supposed."

In that last statement there is much truth. Ibsen was *more* of a poet and *less* a social philosopher than was commonly supposed—less also than others, Bernard Shaw for example, set themselves up to be. He did have tendencies, however, and there really is such a thing as Ibsenism, even though it is less a body of doctrine than enthusiastic disciples tried to make it.

For our purposes, therefore, we are compelled, despite what would probably be his objections, to ask what Ibsen said, in what direction he turned the thoughts and opinions of his audience.

So far as the earliest plays of his mature period are concerned—beginning, let us say, with *The Pillars of Society* in 1877—he first appears and was first taken to be merely a social reformer concerned with specific, rather simple social evils. In *The Pillars of Society* he points out that the rich and powerful are often selfish and corrupt—a thesis not particularly novel even at that date. Approximately two years later *A Doll's House*, the first of his plays to create a sensation, was, on the surface at least, no more than a well-made play involving a plea for "the rights of women" in terms no more advanced than those of John Stuart Mill.

Even in the case of *Ghosts*, Ibsen's next and most deliberately sensational play, what most offended his contemporaries was what they regarded as its shocking indecency, its more than frank treatment of a forbidden topic. An English critic was later to describe it as "a dirty deed done in public," and to many it must have seemed simply shocking rather than in any profound intellectual sense revolutionary. Like *A Doll's House*, it had as its explicit subject a contemporary social problem, but this time it happened to be not the decent question of woman's rights but the indecent problem of venereal disease.

Ibsen's excuse, no doubt, was simply that the very choice of such a subject widened the reach of the play by enabling him to combine the discussion of his specific thesis with a more generalized plea for the discussion of the undiscussable. Many evils, he said, grow like mushrooms in the dark. Oswald Alving, the victim rather than the hero of the play, dies calling out in his insanity, "The sun, Mother, give me the sun," and that was certainly intended to suggest that light rather than decent concealment was what all social evils called for.

Obviously *Ghosts* differed from *A Doll's House* in that the subject was more generalized as well as shocking. The generalization was carried a little further in *An Enemy of the People*, which followed immediately after. This satiric comedy was plainly a reply to Ibsen's critics, and in the course of it he defies all majorities, including that which is called "liberal." Ibsen is announcing that he is not merely a rebel but an archrebel, a rebel who will be, if necessary, against rebels.

The fact remains, nevertheless, that if one saw in the plays no more than what has so far been indicated—and most of his immediate contemporaries probably did not see more at the moment—Ibsen would appear to be not much more than a liberal reformer. One might have granted women equal rights, frankly faced the problem of venereal disease, and even adopted the general principle that it is better to throw light into the dark corners rather than to leave them in what was called decent obscurity, all without having accomplished more than what might reasonably be called "reform." No discontinuity would have necessarily been produced. No chasm would have been opened between the past and the future. What I have tried to suggest as the subject of these discussions would not really have existed at all.

But Ibsen actually went far beyond this, and even in the plays so far mentioned one catches glimpses of concepts far more revolutionary. We have said that *Ghosts* was not merely a play about veneral disease but in general about the "evils that grow in the dark." It is also about a much more revolutionary and dangerous concept.

The title itself suggests at least three levels of meaning.

Inherited disease is a ghost which haunts successive generations of victims. Oswald Alving, making love to the maid Regina, appears to his mother like the ghost of his dissolute father. But the key use of the symbol occurs in the scene where Mrs. Alving argues with her pastor about the proper attitude for her to take toward the whole situation in which she is involved. She and he, she says, are haunted by the ghosts of dead ideas which she sees everywhere about her, even, or perhaps especially, between the lines of what she reads in the newspaper.

In *An Enemy of the People*, speaking the language of comic exaggeration through the mouth of his spokesman, the disillusioned idealist Dr. Stockmann, Ibsen puts into very literal terms what he means. It is not merely that ideas grow stale and platitudinous. One may go one step further and say flatly that truths die. There are no absolute principles of either wisdom or morality. Biblical injunctions such as "Honor thy father and thy mother" as well as political principles such as "The voice of the people is the voice of God" are not simply either true or false. They may have been truths once and falsehoods today. Or as Dr. Stockmann puts it in his excited harangue to his political enemies: "Truths are by no means the wiry Methuselahs some people think them. A normally constituted truth lives—let us say—as a rule, seventeen or eighteen years; at the outside twenty; very seldom more. And truths so patriarchal as that are always shockingly emaciated."

Translated into more abstract terms, what Dr. Stockmann is saying is simply that all truth and all morality are relative—to a situation or to an epoch in history. There are no sure or changeless principles, no truths which can be found and held to, no absolute Right or Wrong to which we can appeal.

Neither Truth, nor Justice, nor Righteousness is fixed outside of time or outside of man. There is no pole star by which we can steer.

Here at last we have reached something that, for the first time, might actually justify talk about a chasm separating the past from the future. A new world which had come to accept an all-inclusive relativity actually would be not merely different from, it would be genuinely discontinuous with an old one in which, on the whole, it was assumed that some unchanging principles were eternally established.

To assume that progress means the accumulation of knowledge, the correction of errors, the winning of a clearer and clearer vision of what Truth has always been, is one thing. That was, for example, Milton's position. Such a definition of progress implies no discontinuity with the past. But to reject, as Ibsen seems to follow Dr. Stockmann in rejecting, the whole concept of Truth as something waiting to be found is another. It cuts the ground out from under one's feet; it digs a chasm into which it is possible to fall, into which it may seem to some that we have actually fallen.

Ibsen boasted that he was no great reader, but neither did he claim absolute originality. What he did say was that a characteristic of the poet is his ability to get new and current ideas out of the atmosphere, without actually reading what his contemporaries are thinking. It often seems as though the poet actually does have this power even though what this means is no more than that, like the inventor who often finds his invention independently and simultaneously worked out by another, the poet is led to certain conclusions by the same historical development which made it possible for writers of whom he is ignorant to announce them. In any event, one of the things which makes Ibsen's work especially suitable for such a discussion as that upon which we are embarking is the fact that in several notable instances he did anticipate other thinkers. It is to these anticipations of highly significant conceptions that we must now turn.

After *An Enemy of the People*, Ibsen's plays became steadily less sociological, more psychological and more metaphysical. He was to end in an almost impenetrable obscurity, although it is at least possible to interpret his last uncompleted play as a defiant declaration that his audiences had never understood what he was about and that it was as well for them that they had not.

Between the sociological plays and the all-too-difficult ones, however, come the three masterpieces *The Wild Duck*, *Rosmersholm*, and *Hedda Gabler*, each of which is subtler than its predecessors and each of which introduces attitudes that widen the chasm between the past and the future.

In *The Wild Duck* there is an "idealist" who continually talks as though he had been reading Ibsen's previous plays, who meddles in the affairs of a strange family, and who produces disastrous results. Living in a house whose closets are chock-full of skeletons, this family has achieved a tolerable *modus vivendi* by ignoring the skeletons and by permitting each member to live in a dreamworld of his own —the feckless father believing himself to be a great inventor, the grandfather dwelling on the past when he was a mighty sportsman, and little Hedvig, the child, centering her emotional life around an attic where a wounded wild duck leads a crippled existence in a make-believe forest.

To the idealist all this appears intolerable. To him as to other admirers of Ibsen it must seem that the whole family is leading a life "based upon a lie." All sorts of evils are "growing in the dark." The remedy is obviously to face facts, to speak frankly, to let in the light. But when the skeletons are brought out of the closet, the whole dreamworld collapses; the weak husband thinks it is his duty to leave his wife, and the little girl, having sacrificed the wild duck, shoots herself with the same gun.

Many of Ibsen's admirers were bewildered. It seemed as though he were taking back everything that in *Ghosts* he had so recently said. It would have been better for all concerned if they had all continued to "live a lie," to choose, not reality, but "a life illusion." To face reality may be to face more than one can bear.

Did Ibsen in *The Wild Duck* mean to say that reality is always more than human nature can endure, that the Truth is the last thing one may hope to live by? If he did, then our discussion is over almost as soon as we have begun it. The conviction that only in a world of things-as-they-are-not can a human being live is a conviction radically pessimistic. It seems, incidentally, to be the one at which Eugene O'Neill arrived in *The Iceman Cometh*. It seems reasonably certain, however, that Ibsen did not really mean that.

Perhaps he did mean to imply that the Truth is only for the strong and that many human beings are weak. But he was also, I think, much more concerned with something else, with a sort of warning to those who thought that he was solving all problems by proclaiming a new set of eternal verities. Ibsenism—in so far as there was any such thing— was not another cult whose principles might be accepted and followed blindly, as the principles of the Church or Positivism or Socialism might be followed. A fool, Ibsen was saying, does not cease to be a fool because he has read *Ghosts*. In other words the moral of the two plays is the same. There is no such thing as an unqualified, unchanging truth. All truths, even Ibsen's, are partial and relative.

That lesson, insisted upon in *Ghosts* and *An Enemy of the People*, must be applied to what those plays themselves say. Mrs. Alving had objected when Parson Manders wanted to fall back upon the injunction "Honor thy father and thy mother" to settle the question whether or not Oswald should be told what kind of man his father had really been. Now the idealist in *The Wild Duck* wants to fall back upon Ibsen's plea for light to settle mechanically the question whether or not the particular family in this play should "face the facts." But Ibsen himself is insisting that Ibsen's plays, like the Holy Scriptures, contain only relative truths. No doubt they too will in time grow stale and become lies. Even in their youth they are true only under certain circumstances. One must not abandon the Bible for Ibsen. There are no infallible teachings.

Rosmersholm is even more treacherously ambiguous because it is easier to miss the ambiguity entirely. In this play the hero is the last of a long line of sternly moralistic landowners. Originally a Christian minister, he has lost faith but hopes to remain firm in the conviction that Christian morality can survive the collapse of its supernatural sanctions. Unfortunately he falls under the influence of Rebecca West, a "new woman" of a type much more advanced and considerably more pretentious than Nora of *A Doll's House*. Rebecca has abandoned not only what may be called the myth of Christianity but, unlike Rosmer, she has abandoned the whole ethical system of Christianity as well. Possibly she may be taken as Ibsen's answer to the still-disputed question of whether or not Christian ethics can be expected to survive the death of the Christian religion.

In any event she has herself gone far beyond the usual

nineteenth-century agnostic. In fact, it is impossible to discuss her without treating her as a Nietzschian before Nietzsche had made his doctrine widely known. She has achieved a transvaluation of values. She has rejected what she does not call but might very well have done so, in Nietzsche's phrase, slave morality. She is for the rights of the strong who have transcended the limitations of those still bound by scruples which are meaningless once one has ceased to believe in the Christian myth that sanctioned them.

Rebecca's secret aim is to marry Rosmer and to lead him on to the step beyond agnosticism which she had taken but which he has not. Without his being aware of her machinations she has led Rosmer's wife to suicide; she is now living in the house with him; and her final success seems imminent. In the last scenes, after he has learned of her responsibility for his wife's death, she leads him to the conviction that they, the two strong individuals, are now completely free to do as they like. Since there is no God in heaven there is nothing outside themselves of which they need to be afraid.

Rosmer seems to agree, but Rebecca does not know how strong the past is, how far he is from having passed over the chasm between the past and the future. Suddenly he finds his solution. Since there is no power *outside* themselves to punish them, they must do justice on themselves. They must punish themselves for their crimes. Rebecca remains icily silent. Presently Rosmer asks her to marry him, and though this has always seemed to be what she wants, she coldly refuses. She goes out and drowns herself in the same stream into which Rosmer's wife has leaped. The past, or "the Rosmer way," has triumphed over the future.

Granted sufficient simplicity of mind, all this might be taken as merely a story of the defeat of evil and the triumph of righteousness. Whatever his personal convictions may have been, Ibsen had grasped the fact that Christian ethics could not easily be carried over the chasm between the past and the future once it had been assumed that the authority of the Christian religion could not be used to fly them across. To Nietzsche he left the task of systematizing an anti-Christian ethic. He was not a philosopher and made no pretense at systematic exposition. But he was a dramatist who sensed the dramatic possibilities of conflicts newly arisen. In this case it meant the dramatic possibilities, not of the conflict between recognized right and recognized wrong, but the conflict between an ethic surviving from the past and an ethic which claimed to prefigure the future.

It is a commonplace that Ibsen's subject matter and his technique produced a revolution in the drama as a literary form. Concerning this I have said nothing and with it I am not immediately concerned. I hope, on the other hand, that what I have already said is sufficient to make obvious just how ominous were his often prophetic insights into the minds of his contemporaries and also the fact that what he was announcing was not merely social change but the disintegration of an intellectual and spiritual world. Before we leave him there is one other point that can best be made in connection with *Hedda Gabler*, which happens to remain, in the contemporary theater, perhaps the most absorbing of his plays.

Once more, as in the case of *A Doll's House* and *Rosmersholm*, the central character is a rebellious woman. But, unlike Rebecca West, Hedda Gabler unambiguously represents some sort of evil. Like Rebecca, she destroys all those who come under her influence, but her destructiveness is naked and intentional, not carried out in the name of something superior which is supposed to take its place. Hedda is plainly sterile and plainly malicious. Her malice is logically pure and disinterested, rather like the malice sometimes attributed to Iago, though the suggestion here is that it arises out of her sterility, that she destroys because she knows she cannot create.

It is true that Hedda often rationalizes her motives. She says that she burns the manuscript of the brilliant but unstable Lövborg because she does not want him to rival her husband. We are aware, however, that this is not really true and that she hates and wishes to destroy the husband also. Sometimes her rationalizations constitute a sort of parody on the genuine motives of Rebecca. Thus when she encourages Lövborg to go to the party where she knows he will succumb to his weakness for drink, she sends him off with the famous injunction, "Come back with vine leaves in your hair," as though she had read Nietzsche and was bidding him achieve some Dionysian splendor. But we know and she knows that he is incapable of any such thing, that her phrase is merely bait to trap him into self-destruction.

Thus, though Rebecca and Hedda seem often to deal in moral or amoral ideas not unrelated to one another, the effect of the two plays is utterly different. It is not merely that the heroine of the second is unmistakably evil while the heroine of the other is allowed to make her case in such a way as to persuade some, at least, that hers is the voice of the future. It is also that, whereas the interest of *Rosmersholm* is intellectual and moral, the interest of *Hedda Gabler* is primarily psychological. In the one case we consider the validity of the heroine's principles and motives; in the other the real question is why she holds them. Rebecca imposes herself as a thinker whether she is right or wrong; Hedda is a kind of case history in abnormal psychology.

Without too much stretching a point, one might also say that whereas *Rosmersholm* anticipates Nietzsche, *Hedda Gabler* anticipates Freud, whose first work on psychoanalysis was published almost a decade later. Hedda is one of the first fully developed neurotic heroines of literature. By that I mean that Hedda is neither logical on the one hand nor, on the other, insane in the old sense of being random and unaccountable. Her aims and her motives have a secret personal logic of their own. She gets what she wants, but what she wants is not anything which the normal usually admit, publicly at least, to be desirable. One of the significant things which such a character implies is the premise that there is a secret, sometimes unconscious, world of aims and methods—one might almost say a secret system of values—that is often much more important than the rational one.

I do not mean to suggest that Ibsen was the first writer to make this assumption in creating a fictional character. No doubt it represents a sort of insight which poets have always occasionally had. Undoubtedly other nineteenth-century writers, Dostoevski especially, provided notable examples of it. But we have agreed to use dramatists as examples, and the example of this particular play is especially clear and striking.

Perhaps I shall not be merely laboring the obvious if I point out how important all this is from the standpoint of any attempt to understand the extent to which there is some justification for considering as unusually drastic the break with the past that Ibsen thought he was making.

If one were looking for a single statement which would suggest, more than any other, the fundamental premise of civilization since Greek times we might do worse than to choose a premise from Aristotle: "Man is a reasoning animal." I do not think that Aristotle meant to say that man never did anything except reason. He was a *reasoning* animal but he was also a reasoning *animal*. Nevertheless, the implication is that reason, or rationality, is the most significant human characteristic. Man is pre-eminently not a creature of instincts or passions or habits or conditioned reflexes but a creature who differs from other animals in the fact that rationality is his dominant mode.

In the older view a man is either sane or insane—sane if he lives chiefly by the light of reason, insane if he rejects it. But what is still sometimes called "the new psychology" breaks down this sharp distinction. It discovers that rationality often plays in the lives of what are called normal people a much smaller part than was once assumed. At the same time it discovers that the abnormal do not act in a merely random, unintelligible manner. There is method in their madness, as there is also usually something like madness in the method of the technically sane. The distinction is a matter of degree. Most men are to some extent neurotic— which means living a sort of double life, partly in reason, partly in unreason. The behavior of Hedda Gabler becomes completely intelligible once one has found the key; but that behavior, though intelligible, is not rational.

Ibsen's understanding of these facts is a poet's intuitive one. He leaves it to Freud to supply clinical evidence. But his pre-Freudian Freudianism is more convincing than that of the playwrights and novelists who base their characterizations and their analysis on the case histories of the psychology books.

Nevertheless, Ibsen can hardly be charged with having done more than open the door. Hedda is presented as an obviously abnormal character. Though she is by far the most interesting person in the play, a sharp distinction is maintained between her and the usually dull but rational characters. She hates the dullness, the timidity, and the conventionality of those whom she destroys, and one of the points which Ibsen seems to be making is that her neurotic revenge is evil, hence to be sharply distinguished from the rational rebellion of his Nora, his Mrs. Alving, and perhaps even his Rebecca West. Ibsen is not, like some of his successors, celebrating the neurotic temperament as superior to the normal one. One can hardly imagine him becoming a surrealist. But he does open the door. With *Hedda Gabler* a deep concern with what is sometimes called "the irrational element" in human life appears as central in a major play by the most influential dramatist of his century.

I shall say less about the "irrational element" now than the subject may seem to demand, largely because I shall return to it in the next chapter in connection with a playwright in whose work it plays an even greater part. In conclusion I should like to note how far-reaching may be the consequences of the concept which Hedda Gabler so strikingly presents.

In a very large proportion of modern literature and even of modern sociology and philosophy, important recognition is accorded the fact that human behavior can be only very imperfectly understood if one proceeds upon the assumption that most men outside the lunatic asylums usually rely upon logical methods to achieve, or attempt to achieve, rationally justifiable ends. Moreover, a very considerable section of our literature and art goes a very long way beyond that. Indeed, some of it seems to assume that the rational is relatively unimportant, that the irrational is usually dominant, and that the richest, most significant aspects of human experience are to be found in the realm of the irrational. Man tends to become less a creature of reason than the victim of obsessions, fixations, delusions, and perversions.

What would Aristotle have made of *Finnegans Wake* or the paintings of Salvador Dali? Suppose that one sets the premise "Man is a rational animal" over against the premise "Man is an irrational animal" or "Man is a conditioned animal." Could any deeper chasm be opened between the past and the future? Ibsen saw that chasm and deepened it.

2 / Strindberg and the
Irreconcilable Conflict

SOME few years ago, in the course of a conversation with Eugene O'Neill, Mr. O'Neill asked me politely about my drama course at Columbia University and what modern playwrights my students found most interesting. To this I replied, "Ibsen among the Europeans and you yourself among the Americans." O'Neill smiled shyly and shook his head. "Ibsen, you say. Ah, I wish it were Strindberg."

That Strindberg was the strongest literary influence on O'Neill is a well-known fact to which O'Neill himself has testified. That Strindberg is also directly or indirectly the strongest literary influence upon the currently admired Tennessee Williams I should be willing to wager. And if I say "direct or indirect," that strengthens rather than weakens the case; for the contention is that, in general, the narrower, more intense, more fanatical spirit of Ibsen's Swedish contemporary, rival, and opponent has been at least as fateful as the influence of Ibsen himself. Many moderns found his passionate, despairing, all-inclusive irrationality more sympathetic and more stimulating than the relatively rational, relatively moderate iconoclasm of Ibsen. Let us consider for a moment what Strindberg did to widen the chasm.

Ibsen was a feminist and a champion of women. Strindberg was an almost insane misogynist. Hatred—or perhaps it was more fear—of women supplies one of the chief motives of his drama despite, or perhaps because of, the fact that he was married three times. In some other respects, nevertheless, Strindberg was less the opposite of Ibsen than an exaggeration of him. In Ibsen his rebelliousness, his sense of isolation, his contempt for the institutions and the spirit of contemporary society, were all kept within some sort of bounds. He mastered them and he used them. Strindberg, on the other hand, was mastered by them and destroyed. Hence, for all the power of his writing, it usually seems to those not completely won over by it shrill and exaggerated. Another way to put it would be to say that Strindberg is far more subjective. Ibsen writes as though he were picturing the world as well as giving his opinion of it. In Strindberg everything seems to be essentially a confession, an intensely personal expression of himself.

Strindberg's youth was passed in bitter poverty and in the bosom of a singularly unhappy family. His own adult life was, if possible, more distracted, and no doubt his view of the typical human lot was to a considerable extent the result of a generalization made from his own. One of his earliest plays, *Sir Bengt's Wife*, which appeared in 1882 and hence shortly after *A Doll's House*, was in some sense an answer to Ibsen's feminist play. In it a husband and wife quarrel for much the same reason that they quarrel in Ibsen's play. But the solution is significantly different. In Ibsen the two part; just before the curtain falls, one hears the sound of the door slammed behind the departing Nora, and it was said that the slamming of that door was heard around the world. In Strindberg's reply, however, the husband and wife achieve a sort of reconciliation although that reconciliation is much more ominous than Nora's running away. They are reconciled, not on any moral or rational basis but because the husband says: "You did not want to love me because your pride forbade it; but you love me anyway. . . . I wanted to hate you; I wished to kill you . . . . but still I love you."

This "reconciliation" is very significant because it anticipates the fundamental attitude expressed in a number of Strindberg's plays, and the problem of the sexes is for him simply a typical example of all human problems. To Strindberg the essence of man's tragic dilemma is that there is no rational, only an irrational, solution of this dilemma. Man is the victim of conflicting desires, and the strongest of them, like his desire for a member of the opposite sex, are irrational and yet stronger than reason. He despises himself for not being able to cease desiring what he also hates.

Ibsen, though recognizing the irrational element, seeks a rational solution. Strindberg passionately, almost hysterically, declares that there is none. In two of his best-known plays, *Countess Julia* and *The Father*, he returns to the specific example afforded by the relation of the sexes. Both plays were written during a period in which he had been encouraged by Zola to think of himself as a scientific naturalist, but both reveal his obsession with subjective convictions.

The first deals with a love-hate relationship·between a noble woman and one of her servants, and it of course reminds us of D. H. Lawrence's notorious *Lady Chatterley's Lover.* In the second, the wife, having driven her husband very near to insanity, actually succeeds in having him committed to an insane asylum.

Since we are concerned not only with the chasm between the past and the future but also with the different conceptions of its essential character and the possibility of crossing it, I think it will be worth while to consider carefully the respective attitudes of Ibsen and Strindberg toward "the woman question." It will illuminate, it seems to me, the question of the approach of these two important dramatists to the whole subject of the irrational element.

That love between the sexes does involve an irrational element is certainly no new discovery. It is at least as old as the legend of the blind cupid. Moreover, moralists have always been concerned with the proper attitude toward this irrational element. In ages when the tendency was to stress almost exclusively the virtues of rationality, love has been thought of as something which reason could and should conquer, so that the Greeks, for instance, sometimes regarded passion as a disease and the English of the eighteenth century depreciated it in favor of something called "rational esteem." In times of more sympathy to mystical ideas, the madness of love is, on the contrary, thought of as a "divine" madness and, by the more extravagant romanticists, as something better, higher, more valuable than anything rational. But it is obvious enough that Strindberg's attitude is significantly different from any of these others, that it is, if you like, a kind of romanticism turned pessimistic.

One may also approach the subject from a different angle.

A consideration of sexual love leads naturally to the question of the differences between man and woman and of their relative worth or importance. A usual attitude in primitive societies seems to be that the difference between them is very great and that women are in general inferior to men. That this was once a prevalent attitude in Greece also may be assumed from the fact that in *The Republic* Plato argues for a modification of it. Women are not to be treated as different from men in their natures or powers. They are to have the same sort of education as men. But they are not to get as much of it because they have less capacity. They are not so much different from men as they are simply lesser men.

One inevitable consequence of this conclusion is that women should be subject to men. They are not to be trusted with authority, even in the home, much less in the state. Neither chivalry nor courtly love, for all their high-sounding talk, change this situation very much. Theoretically, chivalry regarded love as a mystical experience rather than as an unworthy irrationality. Theoretically, woman is deferred to and becomes, half-mockingly, the lover's "mistress," that is, his master. But of course this has nothing to do with practical affairs. Whatever power woman may exercise, it is only the power which man grants her. The metaphysical problem of the worth of sexual love may remain, but there is no open struggle for authority. Medieval or Renaissance Noras do not slam doors heard round the world; there can be no conflict of authority because legally and practically women have no rights.

An extreme but nevertheless logical statement of a later development of the attitude which combines a high value set upon sexual love with an insistence upon the complete subjugation of the female is found in the position of John Milton. Though he is an archpuritan, he is an almost fanatic defender of the significance and holiness of sexual love. Far from being in itself the sin of Adam, it was the crowning delight of life in Paradise before the Fall. When questioned by Adam, the archangel Raphael blushes a rosy red and thus confesses that even in Heaven the angels know it. But woman nevertheless remains in subjugation, and only thus can the irrationality called sexual love be prevented from destroying the rational order of either family or public life. Adam fell because he permitted the irrational element to escape the control of the rational male intelligence. Domestic as well as public peace requires that man's sway should be complete and unquestioned. Man is woman's god. She owes him the same sort of unquestioning obedience which he owes God. Her responsibility is to him as man's responsibility is to the Supreme Being. Any relaxing of the rigor of this principle is fatal. As Samson says in *Samson Agonistes*:

> Therefore God's universal Law
> Gave to man despotic power
> Over his female in due awe,
> Nor from that right to part an hour,
> Smile she or lour:
> So shall he least confusion draw
> On his whole life, not sway'd
> By female usurpation, nor dismay'd.

In practice and in Milton's case the scheme did not, to be sure, work any too well. His Mary, like Ibsen's Nora, ran away although, unlike Nora, she did come back; and we do not have her side of the story. But at least Milton thought that he knew what the right solution of the problem was and, what is more important, he was sure that there was one. On the whole and through all changes the tendency has always been to suppose that the question was one of discovering this right solution. It was not often before the nineteenth century that, as in Strindberg, there was no solution.

Victorians rather tended to hold to the idea that men and women were very different creatures, but they also at least pretended to believe that women were in their own way superior—in sensitivity, that is, and especially in purity. They denied women sway, not on the ground that they were inferior, but on the ground that their superior delicacy and purity must be protected. Men were to do the rough work, which included being the master in all practical affairs, in order that women might escape the coarsening contact of the world.

What the woman movement meant, from Mary Godwin through John Stuart Mill, was half a return to Plato's theory that men and women are not different in their natures. But it rejected at the same time the assumption that they were lesser. Men and women were declared to be essentially alike both in their natures and in their powers. It is not man's exclusive right to rule, and woman's business is not to be either submissive on the one hand or the source of merely romantic inspiration on the other. She has equal rights and responsibilities as well as much more nearly similar duties than was previously supposed. Marriage should be the partnership of equals.

This seems to be much the position which Ibsen takes in *A Doll's House*. If Nora had been given the same education as a man, if her husband had taken her into his confidence, if he had treated her in every respect as his equal and shared his responsibilities with her, all would have been well. There is a solution to the problem of the marital relationship, and enlightenment will find it. Full partnership is the key to the problem. Fundamentally, then, A Doll's House is a very, perhaps almost naively, optimistic play.

The purpose of this rather lengthy digression is, of course, to emphasize what is radically novel in Strindberg's attitude —namely, his conviction that the woman problem is completely unsolvable. Men and women are different, and this means both that they want different things and that each is determined to dominate. If one could conquer the other, then some sort of peace based on subjugation might be achieved. If either could be as consistently ruthless as he sometimes is willing to be, then he might achieve such a peace. But irrational love, the desire and need of one for the other, makes this impossible. Men and women can neither consistently love nor consistently hate. Each is condemned to a hell of conflict and frustration until one or the other is destroyed. Man is too irrational a creature ever to achieve a rational order even in his personal life.

I must confess that I do not know who first used the phrase "the battle of the sexes." In any event Strindberg is as much responsible as anyone for the popularization of the conception behind the phrase, and it is now a very familiar one. Bernard Shaw gives his own optimistic version in Man and Superman, and few discussions of the "sex problem" fail to assume that the phrase represents some reality which plays a part in, even if it does not constitute the whole of, that problem. A few years ago James Thurber did an amusing series of drawings representing "The War between Men and Women" in terms of an actual military campaign, and the pictures would have had no point if the average reader of The New Yorker had not been familiar with "the battle of the sexes."

The significant fact about Strindberg, however, is not simply that he popularized the assumption that some sort of sex rivalry is inevitable. Not only did he make irreconcilable conflict the central fact in the relation between men and women but also, by analogy, he made it the central fact in the whole problem of the good life. No good life in the classical sense is possible because a good life would demand the resolution of conflicts which can never be resolved. The woman problem is not only basic; it is also typical of the whole human dilemma.

To make dissonance rather than harmony the condition to which the human universe naturally tends and the condition to which it is inevitably condemned is to accept as a premise a view of man's state and of his destiny sufficiently novel to justify once more the contention that a chasm has yawned between the past and the future. In connection with the subject it is perhaps worth while to point out a curious analogy between Strindberg's insistence that war is the inevitable condition of any intimate relationship between men and women and a somewhat similar novelty in the economic thought of the nineteenth century.

Most theories of the state have assumed that some sort of Justice with a capital J is possible and that in a well-governed society the interests of all classes are harmonized. Even the theory of the divine right of kings assumed that absolute rule brought some kind of "greatest good for the greatest number." In the moderate eighteenth century, Dr. Johnson spoke for Toryism when he discoursed on the generally beneficent effect of "the great scheme of subordination." Classical economics assumed that *laisser faire* provided as well as it was possible to provide for the interests of both the employer and the employed. Indeed, some of the early nineteenth-century economists went to what seems to us absurd lengths in justifying their contention that even when it seemed to work hardships upon the laboring classes it was nevertheless providing them with as much as the resources of the world could possibly provide. And even the severer critics of prevailing conditions commonly assumed that some harmony of interests could be achieved.

Karl Marx's theory of the class war represents a theory as radical and as revolutionary in its field as the Strindbergian or Thurberian sex wars. Love and work represent, perhaps, the two most important fields of human concern, and in connection with both an influential writer of the nineteenth century introduces a similar revolutionary concept and insists that all attempts to achieve a rational harmony are doomed to failure because the central eternal reality is not a community of interests but a conflict of interests. Marx, to be sure, does hope for one sort of solution. The conflict can be abolished by the abolition of one of the conflicting interests. The class war will cease when there is no longer more than one class. But no such happy solution of Strindberg's dilemma is possible. It hardly seems practicable to suggest that one of the sexes be abolished. We must therefore face the fact that the world is and will continue to be simultaneously occupied by implacable enemies. The personal life of a human being can never be a harmony; it must always remain a discord.

Like Ibsen, Strindberg influenced the form as well as the tone and mood of the drama. As I have already indicated, he at one time thought of himself as a practitioner of Zola's naturalism, and both *Countess Julia* and *The Father* are in a more or less naturalistic form. But as he grew more frantic and apocalyptic he threw off the pseudoscientific, pseudo

objectivity of naturalism and developed a visionary sub-
jectivism most typically represented by *The Dream Play*, in
which the logic and the mechanisms of the dream state are
used to make comments upon human life, with special
stress upon its irrationality.

This particular play is generally and probably properly
credited with being the precursor of the whole nonrepre-
sentational modern drama, including Italian futurism, post–
World War I "expressionism" in Germany, and the
experimental theater of the Russian twenties and thirties.
Certain of O'Neill's plays, notably *The Hairy Ape*, show its
influence and so do many other American experimental plays
including Elmer Rice's once famous *The Adding Machine*.

No sort of consistency, however, either of thought or of
method is to be expected of Strindberg, who is always vio-
lent and extreme. At one period he turns Christian and
writes of resignation and Christian piety. But the center,
or rather the vortex, to which he tends to return always
involves irrational and unresolvable conflict.

Of Ibsen's last moments a story is told which is humorously significant. It is said that just before he died he raised
his head from the pillow to say one word: "Nevertheless"—
and trailed off into silence. This anecdote ought to be true
whether it is or not because Ibsen had a "neverthelessing"
mind. When he seems to take opposite points of view, as in
Ghosts and *The Wild Duck*, it is not inconsistency but reser-
vation and qualification. Nothing stated simply and unreserv-
edly is completely true. One must look at the other side as it
presents itself under other circumstances.

Strindberg, on the contrary, does not qualify. His temperament is the believing temperament, not the skeptical
one. He changes his mind and goes wholeheartedly from

one extreme position to the other. Hence he can write nihilistic plays or he can write Catholic plays. But there is little place for a "nevertheless" in either. The thing that is most original and powerful is what you get when the pendulum swings all the way, as it does in *The Father*, *The Dream Play*, or, to mention another of the "expressionistic" works, *The Ghost Sonata*.

The last two probably represent most completely the desperation to which he is led by the conviction that man is torn between irreconcilable impulses and that the universe itself puts him on the horns of a dilemma. It is not merely that in both the central characters are frustrated and destroyed, that their hopes and plans are defeated. All the hopes and plans of man must be frustrated because they involve impossible reconciliations, of which the need to reconcile the hatred of man for woman with the desire of one for the other is an example. The only conclusion to be reached is that enunciated by the goddess in *The Dream Play* which is simply, "Men are pitiable creatures."

In the Greek drama also men are, among other things, pitiable creatures. But they are that only "among other things." In the finest and best-known Greek tragedies men are also guilty creatures. They suffer through faults in their character. They do irrational or wrong things; especially, perhaps, they permit themselves the sin of pride. In Strindberg, on the other hand, no fault is necessary beyond the fault of being a man, and hence no hope or remedy can be held out, no usable injunction issued. How but irrationally can man possibly behave when to be a man at all is, by definition, to be more irrational than rational.

There is only one step further into the chasm that Strindberg can take. Happiness as well as peace must be rejected, not only as a possible but also even as a desirable end. In this decision he seems again to approach the philosophical formula of Nietzsche. Though he does not use Nietzsche's terms, the Dionysian and the Apollonian, he illustrates them, and we may as well take up the terms here because recent speculators, especially certain anthropologists, have taken them up and given them rich contexts.

In art, in ethics, in any given culture as a whole, the Apollonian has been taken to represent all aspirations in the direction of rationality, harmony, peace, contentment, and quiet happiness. Apollonianism is co-operative, uncompetitive, serene. In a word, it holds that harmony should and can rule both in society and within the individual. But in man and therefore in nearly every society, there is also a Dionysian or drunken element. It promotes not only contest, rivalry, and strife, but also the intoxication of heroism, the ecstasy of pain and of self-destruction. It scorns mere happiness in favor of adventure, the sense of power, the exultation of struggle, even if it is a death struggle. In civilized societies it sends men not only to war but to dangerous sports such as mountain climbing. In primitive societies it inspires strange religious rites, including the orgies of masochism and sadism, the reverence for the priest who is either epileptic or drugged. To seek contentment and peace is rational and therefore to the worshiper of Dionysus not really human. To seek difficulty, pain, and madness is irrational and therefore peculiarly human. These things reveal the nature of man; rationality is only something which he tries unsuccessfully to impose upon himself. If happiness is unobtainable, some sort of fulfillment in the Dionysian orgy is. If life is to be regarded as in any sense good, then it must be that it is "good because it is painful." In that statement man's irrationality finally reaches full expression of itself through a pronouncement which irrationally reconciles two irreconcilables, "the good" and "the painful." "Moderation in all things" is the fundamental doctrine of the Apollonian. Blake's "The road of excess leads to the palace of wisdom" is its opposite.

To contemplate these conclusions which are at least foreshadowed in Strindberg is to be reminded how rational, how nearly tame and conventional by comparison Ibsen seems to be. Nor is this merely a matter of appearance. Ibsen may have approached the edge of a chasm or abyss, but he did not, like Strindberg, fall into it.

Ibsen's personal life was calm and regular. Indeed, up to the time when a paralytic stroke, followed by amnesia, put a final end to his career, he seemed outwardly to become more and more respectable as well as more and more prosperous—in many respects the typical substantial bourgeois. Though he was by many regarded as a dangerous radical, the surface of his life was irreproachable. In his old age this enemy of the people looked very much like a clergyman of one of the sterner Protestant sects. As his world fame grew, he began to be regarded by his fellow countrymen as a national hero, to whom, as a matter of fact, a state funeral was given when at last he died.

Nor was all this merely a matter of outward appearance. In the previous chapter I stressed the revolutionary aspects of his attitudes. But when one looks back at him after considering the work of his Danish rival, one becomes aware of certain conservative tendencies that take on a special importance in the light of subsequent developments in the drama and in modern thought.

For one thing, certain of his plays are social or, perhaps

better, reformist plays. At least *A Doll's House, Ghosts,* and *An Enemy of the People* are concerned with social evils apparently regarded as remediable. In that sense they are optimistic: at least they do not represent either man or society as placed in some hopeless dilemma. Ibsen speaks as though "more light" could actually be expected to banish most of the evils which "grow in the dark."

Moreover, to consider a negative aspect, Ibsen does not, like Strindberg, surrender to the irrational element. He recognizes the part which it plays in human life; in one play, *Hedda Gabler,* he presents us with a character who has entirely submitted to it. But that character is neither admirable nor represented as typical. There is no suggestion that mankind must or should surrender his rationality. There remains, therefore, an element—and to me it seems the dominant element—which is Apollonian rather than Dionysian.

Nowhere is there the suggestion which one will find not only in Strindberg but in other Dionysians—D. H. Lawrence, for example—that the only salvation for man is a kind of accepted damnation, that life is good because it is painful.

Moreover, Ibsen's conservatism has also a positive aspect which can be simply stated. He was always and above all an individualist and a moralist. He might doubt the existence of unchanging moral absolutes or at least doubt the possibility of formulating them in codes. But his universe is a moral universe to which the individual must adapt himself, and his final judgments are always judgments passed upon an individual who either acts or fails to act in accordance with what one is tempted to call in religio-moralistic terms his "inner light."

Bernard Shaw, who did more than any other one man to introduce Ibsen to the English-speaking world, also did all he could to obscure this fact. His little book *The Quintessence of Ibsenism* was the first important interpretation of Ibsen in English, and it might much better have been called *The Quintessence of Shavianism* because Shaw is always more concerned with what he thought Ibsen ought to have said than with what Ibsen actually did say. Shaw was anxious to make him appear less a moralist in any old-fashioned sense than the preacher of a doctrine which could be reconciled with the young Shaw's own socioeconomic determinism. In *The Perfect Wagnerite* Shaw succeeded in interpreting *The Ring of the Nibelungen* as a Marxian allegory of the decline of capitalism. A man who did that would obviously have no great difficulty in misinterpreting Ibsen.

In the light of subsequent intellectual developments it is, as a matter of fact, rather difficult not to misinterpret Ibsen. After all, he was an early leader of the "modern" movement. Certain concepts have come to seem very characteristic of that movement. Ergo, they must have been present in Ibsen's plays. But if, without prejudice, one examines the plays themselves, one perceives not only that many characteristic dogmas of the several different "modernisms" are not there but that their opposites often are. As one looks back it sometimes seems that Ibsen has come to be a voice from the past, that he himself has remained on the far side of the chasm which others have attempted to cross.

Thus, although he became one of the heroes of the political modernists, he never had much faith in political action and never belonged to any political party. Somewhat defiantly he referred to himself as an aristocrat, and though that is not to be taken to mean that he had great faith in the virtue of ability of an actual aristocracy, it does mean that he had, if possible, even less faith in the "liberal majority." In some sense he may have been a democrat, but he was certainly not one in the sense, common today, of one who has faith in the common man or who believes that mediocrity and ordinariness are admirable and valuable. He would never, like Gerhart Hauptmann in *The Weavers*, have made a class rather than a particular man or woman the protagonist of a play. His interest was always in the extraordinary individual. In so far as he was hopeful, what he obviously believed in was not the mass but the saving remnant.

What is most important, however, in connection with the special concern of these discussions is the fact that he was, as I said a little earlier, pre-eminently a moralist. By this I mean, first, that moral success or failure seems to him the most important thing in the world and that it is by their moral success or failure that he judges his characters. It means, second, that despite his criticism of social institutions he never shifts the burden of responsibility from the individual to "social conditions" or economic pressures.

It is an axiom which seems to be accepted today by almost every species and shade of liberal that society makes men and that when we are what we ought not to be the institutions of our society are ultimately responsible. But the old-fashioned view of Ibsen unmistakably is not that men are made by the society in which they live, but that society is made by the men who live in it and that the defects of man's institutions are the result of defects in him—not the other way around. If this is a hypocritical, unjust, stupid, and cruel society, it is such because it is the society which has been willed by hypocritical, unjust, stupid, and cruel men. If it is ever to be better, it will have to become so because better men have made it.

That this actually was his position can be made clear by the analysis of any one of the distinctly "social" plays but most easily, perhaps, in connection with the most famous, *Ghosts*. Of this play it has been wrongly said that the hero is Oswald Alving, the helpless victim of hereditary disease, and that the tragic fault lies in the society which concealed the true character of his father and which was ultimately responsible for his existence because its pressures compelled Mrs. Alving to live with Oswald's father and to beget Oswald himself. Actually the real protagonist is not the helpless victim Oswald but his mother; the tragic guilt is, ultimately, not that of society but of the protagonist herself because she listened to Parson Manders in whom she did not really believe and because she submitted to the opinion of the community instead of following her own inward light which told her, from the beginning, that what she was doing was wrong. Before the play is over she asserts herself and earns the right to be called a heroine when she finally rejects the hypocritical morality preached by society and does what she herself believes to be right. It is too late to prevent the evils which her earlier wrongdoing had created. Therefore, as is so often the case in tragedy, the hero achieves a triumphant clarification though he can no longer save either himself or the others.

Thus Mrs. Alving was not, as many would say today, the victim of the society in which she lived. Ibsen says clearly that it is the duty of a moral man to resist society when it is wrong and that this is what members of the saving remnant do. The hope for mankind lies with those who refuse, as the strong man can refuse, to be "the product of social forces."

Ibsen's conservative insistence upon individual responsibility, upon the ability of the individual actually to make
choices and thus to direct his own destiny, serves to set him
in opposition to two tendencies in modernism. In the first
place, as we shall see when we come to consider Bernard
Shaw, the eclectic, Ibsenism is fundamentally anti-Marxian
and is contrary to even the somewhat diluted Marxian doctrine found in almost all varieties of liberalism because it
assumes that the individual, not the social group, is the determining factor. Ibsen bids every man reform himself before he attempts to reform society. In the second place, this
same insistence implies a faith both in some sort of free
will and in the possibility that reason can be made to dominate over irrationality. There is in the individual an "I"
which can effectively say to itself, "I make this choice; I am
determined to act in this way." Moreover, the choice of that
"I" can be a rational choice.

Perhaps the whole thing may be summed up as follows.
Most modern sociology, relying upon economics and psychology, proposes to build a new bridge across the chasm
which separates the past from the future and to carry us
safely across to some happier land where we shall all be
cheerful and prosperous because a just society and a per-
fected technique for adjusting the soul to its environment
will make us cheerful and prosperous, willy-nilly. Ibsen, despite all that he discards, seems to hold fast to old-fashioned
concepts which will carry us across if anything will—namely,
to a belief in rationality as a determining factor in life and
a belief in free will by means of which at least the excep-
tional, heroic individual can save both himself and, ultimately perhaps, the mass of mankind.

Strindberg, believing in the practicability of no bridges, simply invites us to plunge with him into the abyss. While Ibsen recognizes the existence of the irrational element and in *Hedda Gabler* acknowledges the possibility that in a given individual it may become completely dominant, the normal man nevertheless remains for him the predominantly rational man. Strindberg, on the other hand, seems to say: "Man is an irrational animal. It is his irrationality, not his rationality, which distinguishes and defines him. To be a man at all is to be neurotic, self-destructive, and unhappy."

This last doctrine is not one which lends itself very readily to systematic exposition and evangelistic advocacy. But the importance of its influence should not be minimized for that reason. A certain kind of play or novel or poem very readily conveys it. It comes easily to color or give the emotional tone to a certain sort of confused, catastrophic story which an age without faith is very likely to find itself telling. As I have already indicated, one most often finds Strindbergism in solution rather than crystallized as a dogma in such popular American dramatists as Eugene O'Neill and Tennessee Williams. Moreover, despite the quasi-theological dogma to which they are formally committed, one may also find it strong in the writings of the French existentialists. In fact, there are comparatively few modern works of serious pretensions in which one is likely to find a hero who fulfills completely the conditions of Aristotle's definition. Nearly all seem to proclaim that man is, to a sometimes lesser and sometimes greater degree, an irrational animal.

3 / Bernard Shaw and the Inadequate Man

ONE EVENING in 1892, the first of Oscar Wilde's four successful comedies had in London its first performance. It is said that after the last curtain the audience rose to cheer—and it had good reason to do so. Not in several generations had a new play so sparkled with fresh and copious wit of a curiously original kind.

By now the play itself, *Lady Windermere's Fan*, seems thin and faded. To be successfully revived, as it was a few seasons ago in the United States, it has to be presented as "a period piece"—which means that the audience is invited to laugh at as well as with it. Paradoxically, the only thing about it which can be taken seriously today is its fun, intentional as well as, occasionally, unintended. Few remember long what the story is about. But a dozen such epigrams as "There is nothing like the love of a married woman; it is something no married man knows anything about" are in quotation books and still pass in current conversation. It would probably be not too much of an exaggeration to say that it was the first theatrically successful English play since Sheridan to win a place in English literature. If, in English drama, we are to look for what we have been calling modernism, we can hardly do better than to start with *Lady Windermere's Fan.*

Wilde had, of course, already made himself famous, or at least notorious, in other ways and had become the best-known specimen of the new, irritating kind of writer called an aesthete. He had been delightedly shocking the public by proclaiming that the chief end of man is not the pursuit of Truth or of Virtue but of Beauty—which often found itself the enemy of both Truth and Virtue and which sometimes degenerated into mere Pleasure, sometimes trivial and sometimes forbidden. Wilde had not, himself, invented or even significantly developed any part of the doctrine. He had borrowed it partly from Walter Pater, who had taught at Oxford when Wilde was a student there, and partly from France, where aestheticism, known also as decadence, had already run a long course from Gautier down to Wilde's own contemporary Huysmans. He had published poems which *Punch* accurately described as "Swinburne and water." With a somewhat greater success he had also published the sensational prose tale *The Picture of Dorian Gray,* which was obviously inspired by Huysmans and in which a great deal of wit was mingled with a good deal of nastiness. Besides all that, he had written as well the "aesthetic" tragedy *Salomé,* forbidden performance by the Lord Chamberlain. With a great talent for publicity, he was, however, better known as a personality than as a writer and as such was known to thousands who had never read him.

Inevitably, when Gilbert and Sullivan decided to write an opera on the subject of the aesthetic poet, they made the hero dress in the knee breeches and silk stockings which were part of Wilde's favorite costume, and they made various allusions to his supposed behavior. To all this Wilde delightedly gave his unofficial collaboration. There is even some reason to believe that he may have been aware of the fact that the American lecture tour arranged for him by Gilbert and Sullivan's own agents was partly a publicity stunt to advertise in the United States the subject of the opera. Wilde simply accepted the publicity and depended upon his wit to escape the possibility that he might become merely a butt. He denied, for example, that he had ever walked down Piccadilly stopping from time to time to gaze with aesthetic rapture at the lily which he carried in his hand. Anyone, he said, could have done that. He did something much more difficult. Without ever having "walked down Piccadilly with a tulip or a lily in his medieval hand," he had made people believe that he had. Asked what he thought of *Patience*, he replied that "Parody is the tribute which mediocrity pays to genius." He thought that that single remark left the victory on his side. And I am not sure that it did not.

Lady Windermere's Fan was followed by three other comedies of which the last, *The Importance of Being Earnest*, was the most consistent, the most sustained, and the best. They were the first genuinely popular successes to be achieved by a man who had previously been "well disliked" rather than "well liked." Moreover, they represent the successful exploitation of a discovery which Wilde had previously made, namely that aestheticism, which was merely pretty-pretty in some of his poems, rather horrible in *Salomé,* and rather nasty in *The Picture of Dorian Gray,* could be employed to supply the paradoxical element in an original brand of wit.

Perhaps Wilde himself was never sure just how seriously he took the aesthetic doctrine. Possibly this fact accounts for the terrible catastrophe which finally destroyed him when he took it more literally than he had intended. In any event he had always had a great, unexpected sense of sheer fun; in the comedies he gave it rein, using intellectual and moral perversity only to add a certain spice.

When one character remarks, "Twenty years of romance make a woman look like a ruin," and when he pauses a moment before adding, "But twenty years of marriage make her look like a public building," one is aware chiefly of the glorious absurdity of the metaphors, the quick play upon the derogatory and the favorable senses of the word "ruin." If one permits oneself to be absurdly solemn on the subject, one may say that the standard of values implied is the standard of aestheticism, since the moral choice between "romance" and "marriage" is dismissed in favor of the superior importance of the aesthetic results respectively attributed to the respectable and the disreputable courses of conduct.

Or, to take another example, when a character returning from the conservatory describes an orchid by saying, "It is as beautiful as the seven deadly sins," that is both a very witty description of the exotic, extravagant, almost repellent beauty of the particular class of blossom and also—if one wants to take it this way—the equivalent of the play *Salomé,* where the stress is upon the special kind of beauty which the deadly sins are declared to reveal.

Of course comedy does not need to take it this way. The

thing is an epigram, not a moral precept, and an epigram has been very profoundly as well as epigrammatically defined as "a half-truth so stated as to be especially irritating to those who believe the other half." Wit is largely a matter of half-truths, of usually rather disillusioning, rather tough-minded half-truths, irritating to the unrelievedly idealistic. And aestheticism, even perversity and decadence, often supply these corrective half-truths. There was enough acid in Wilde's epigrams to dissolve a good deal of what we call Victorianism. Victorianism was one small, local aspect of that Past which Ibsen saw as the enemy of the Future. Wilde made, therefore, his small contribution to the development of "modernism." We shall see presently why, even among English dramatists, he is nevertheless not one of "modernism's" most important spokesmen.

Everyone interested in either the theater or literature was aware of the Wilde comedies during their brilliant runs. On the contrary, only a few zealots noticed that, a year or two before, an *avant-garde* group produced A *Doll's House*, the first Ibsen play ever seen in England. A year or two after that, *Ghosts* aroused the ire of drama critics, some of whom saw in it nothing except a crude and deliberate offense against decency, and before long "Ibsenism" was a term which had begun to be bandied about in advance circles. But it was quite a while before any very large public was as fully aware of "Ibsenism" as it was already aware of a "aestheticism," because aestheticism seemed to be the really important contemporary school.

For one thing, it was coherently organized. It had magazines, successively *The Yellow Book* and the *Savoy*, which were hospitable to its practitioners. And besides its showman, Wilde, it had Ernest Dowson as poet, Aubrey Beardsley as artist, Arthur Symons as critic. Certainly the average conservative Englishman, ever alert to the threat which unconventional art was always raising against sound morality and good form, saw the aesthetes as the most important current embodiment of the enemy. He was alarmed at the spreading taste for what Tennyson, speaking of Swinburne, had called "poisonous honey brought from France." He was not yet very much aware of the dark northern cloud gathering on the horizon. He half feared that his world was going to be corrupted by the effeminacy and vice which were supposed to accompany the cult of Beauty; he did not realize that what really threatened late Victorianism was not soft decadence but something much more drastic—the thing which Nietzsche had called "the transvaluation of values" and of which we have seen examples in Ibsen and Strindberg. Before long, aestheticism would become simply "old hat" and its heyday humorously, condescendingly, almost affectionately, dismissed as the "naughty nineties." So far as England is concerned, modernism in literature and specifically in the drama had simply got off to a false start.

The reasons why aestheticism failed as an effective revolutionary movement are no doubt many. The most obvious outward one was the dreadful scandal which dragged Wilde down to destruction and which made everyone in any way associated with him suspect, if not worse. The movement could not survive Wilde's disgrace. But there is also a deeper reason which was cogently stated by Bernard Shaw, who became, for England, the great expounder of Ibsen, of Nietzsche, of Marx and the whole genuinely revolutionary crew. That deeper reason is simply this. Man is an incorrigibly moral animal. Wickedness, even when presented as attractively as the aesthetes presented it, never destroys a morality, or at least a moral theory. The only dangerous threat to an established morality is a new morality. It was, of course, in the guise of a new morality that the opinions of Ibsen, of Nietzsche, and of Marx presented themselves. These men did not say, "Let us be naughty." They said, "Let us be good"; not "Let us pervert values," but "Let us transvaluate them." They did not talk about splendid sins but about new virtues.

First as pamphleteer and critic, then as playwright, Bernard Shaw was soon to become the most important "new playwright" in the English-speaking world and also one of the most important literary exponents of modernism in any form. Like all the important dramatists who may be called followers of Ibsen, he did much more than merely follow; despite his indebtedness, his plays are vastly different in form, in general effect, and in doctrine from those of Ibsen. Since we are to use him as one of our key figures in our attempt to discover through the drama some of the things which the conception of a chasm between the past and the future means, a few generalizations about Shaw are necessary.

Ibsen was commonly referred to as "the gloomy Scandinavian," but there was nothing gloomy about his young British defender. Moreover, though Shaw was a contemporary of Wilde in London, there was nothing aesthetic about him either. He was dressed, not in the knee breeches and silk stockings of Gilbert's Bunthorne, but in virile tweeds surmounted by a flaming red beard. Decidedly there was nothing lilylike or languishing about him. Moreover, his head was filled, not with Pater and Swinburne and

Huysmans and the rest, but with the doctrines of revolutionary socialism and with the latest philosophical ideas about the workingman.

Next to his optimism and his energy, the most striking thing about Shaw was his furious eclecticism. He felt no necessity to choose between the various modern prophets. He would take something from them all, and moreover he would reconcile the most disparate. He was an Ibsenite of course. But he was also, or was soon to become, a disciple of Marx, of Nietzsche, of Bergson, of Wagner, of Samuel Butler, and of John Bunyan. Besides becoming a socialist, he was also a nonsmoker, a teetotaler, a vegetarian, an antivaccinationist, an antivivisectionist and an advocate of reformed spelling.

All this would have been more than enough to give a serious case of intellectual indigestion to anyone else, but for him it was merely very stimulating and very nourishing. Sooner or later the teaching of all his masters was synthesized, one furnishing an economic system, another a moral system, a third a metaphysic, and a fourth a religion. Though he never wrote it all down in systematic form, Shaw has at one time or another propounded the parts of what is probably the most inclusive body of doctrine since Thomas Aquinas.

One thing which made this possible was a sort of cheerful optimism enabling him to temper the more intransigent doctrines of his various masters and to fall back upon the formula "What this really means is . . ." Moreover, what it really meant was usually something less intransigent as well as frequently gentler and more kindly than the doctrine of his masters is generally assumed to be.

In the plays of the first decade especially, this cheerful

determination to tame the wild men and to draw the fangs of revolution seems particularly striking. Nietzsche's doctrine of the superman—which might seem to others to foreshadow a blond beast, amoral and ruthless—tends to become no more than a rather extravagant method of recommending self-help and improvement. *The Revolutionist's Handbook*, supposed to have been written by the rebellious John Tanner, hero of *Man and Superman*, begins by breathing fire and then carefully explains that in democratic England there is all the revolution necessary every time the voters have recourse to the ballot box. In the same book a shocking section ridiculing sexual morality and especially the sentimental word "purity" ends by demonstrating that, since the number of men and women in England is approximately equal, monogamy is the only sensible system. In that same play even Strindberg's battle of the sexes, described by Tanner in the first scene as a remorseless struggle where the only question is which party shall destroy the other, turns out to be but a sort of sham battle in the course of which the Life Force makes the hero and heroine temporarily irrational in order that it may benevolently trick them into sacrificing what they believe to be their desires in favor of their deepest impulse—which is to try to create better offspring.

In Tanner's last exuberant comic speech in which he rejects the impending congratulation incident to the announcement of his engagement, he proclaims, "This is not happiness but the price for which the strong sell their happiness." This is, if you like, an ingenious comic perversion of the doctrine that life is good because it is painful. But the whole tone and meaning are something quite different. It comes down to little more than a version of the ancient joke on the Benedict who ruefully protests that he has not changed his ideas a bit but that somehow he finds himself not too sorry that he is about to become Benedict the married man after all. Thus the early Shaw, having delightedly absorbed the leading revolutionary ideas of late-nineteenth-century Europe, attempts to reinterpret them with typical English moderation. Radicals of our day are fond of apologizing for invasions, executions, enslavements, and the like by saying that "you cannot make a revolution without breaking a few eggs." The early Shaw seemed resolved to do just that. To what extent he ultimately succeeded we shall see presently.

Though Shaw was simultaneously serving many gods, the most powerful influence upon his young maturity was one which Ibsen and Strindberg felt feebly if at all. His own statement is categorical: Marx made a man of me. Before he read *Das Kapital* in the British Museum where it had been conceived, Shaw had already embraced quite a variety of heresies, but they were separate and disorganized. Marx's doctrine gave him a center around which the other dogmas could be arranged. He had now a system, wrong in details as he was to proclaim, and incomplete until Nietzsche, Bergson, and the rest had been integrated into it, but fundamental, nevertheless. "Marxian" was the most definite and unequivocal label which he was willing to wear.

This meant that though he might extol Ibsen as a dramatic artist and expound various of his ideas, Shavianism must necessarily be in some respects the antithesis of Ibsenism. Inevitably a Marxist must shift a good deal of the emphasis from the moral to the economic. Men are much more the product of economic forces, much less the result of what their free moral decisions make them, than Ibsen seems to assume. Politics becomes at least as important as personal integrity, which, indeed, is almost useless without it. Thus while Ibsen remains outside all parties, Shaw becomes an active Fabian socialist. He advocates, as Ibsen does not, a program. And with this go various important shifts of emphasis. Shaw proclaims that a good writer is inevitably a propagandist. The great Englishman of letters is not Shakespeare but Bunyan. Whereas Ibsen could say, "I have been more of a poet and less of a social philosopher than has commonly been supposed," Shaw on the contrary will emphasize his didactic intention and at times go so far as to say that he wrote his plays only because he happened to discover that when writing in play form he drew the largest audience. Above all Shaw would never have said, "My business is to ask questions, not to answer them." In fact, he cheerfully set himself up as an oracle to whom all the answers were accessible. Or, as a character in one of his later plays announces: "I can explain anything to anybody. And what is more I enjoy doing it."

Perhaps the toughest question which he finds himself called upon to answer is how economic determinism, taken from Marx, is to be reconciled with Shaw's own moral preference for the doctrine of free will and of the duty of every individual to struggle toward his ideal of the Superman. Shaw's religion—what he calls his metabiology—is drawn largely from evolutionary theories and from the philosophy of Bergson. It assumes that, just as man emerged from some apelike ancester, so he will in time give rise to a Superman by comparison with whom the man of today will seem no more than a sort of ape. But he indignantly rejects, on purely moral grounds, the Darwinian theory which assumes that natural selection has simply pushed organisms willy-nilly along the evolutionary road. It is therefore on moral grounds that he sturdily proclaims himself not a Darwinian, but a Lamarckian—one, that is to say, who believes that the will to improvement is the dynamic element in progress. The giraffe, as he says in one place, did not get a long neck because the giraffes which happened to have rather longish necks survived better. It got a long neck because successive generations *wanted* long necks. According to him the two great forces in evolution are the imagination and the will. The imagination dreams dreams, and the will determines that the dream shall come true.

It is an attractive idea, but it seems to run counter to Marx if Marx really is an economic determinist. To many, at least, Marxism seems indeed a rather exact economic equivalent of Darwinism. Darwin teaches that animals simply have to evolve, Marx that societies simply have to do the same thing. Shaw seems determined to insist that both are somehow true —that man is the product of society but that he is also, somewhat inexplicably, the master of his destiny. In the later plays the mystical element grows stronger and stronger, but in the beginning he appears primarily as a Marxian or perhaps neo-Marxian critic of social and economic institutions.

To answer questions as Shaw proposed to do takes much more time than merely, like Ibsen, to ask them. Notoriously he found it increasingly difficult to crowd what he had to say into plays if they were to retain any semblance at all of being plays. Accordingly he got into the habit of writing prefaces often longer than the plays and frequently so full and interesting that they almost made the plays unnecessary. Add the various expository books, the controversial articles, and so forth, and Shaw may well be the most voluminous writer since Voltaire. There were few subjects upon which he was not prepared to say the final word.

Even to outline his principal dogmas, attitudes, and preferences would require a whole series of discussions devoted to nothing else. Fortunately for our special purposes nothing of this sort is necessary. I must remind you again that my concern is with the concept of the chasm between the past and the future, with the way in which certain dramatists conceived that chasm, and with the extent to which they succeeded in making the Future seem a humanly livable realm. So far as Shaw is concerned, my thesis is that, optimist though he was and in a sense professed to remain, he also ran into increasing difficulties and ended with a view of the future not very attractive to most of us. I think that I can illustrate this thesis rather briefly by considering, first, two plays which represent two stages in the development of his ideas about government, then one later play which professed to sum up his metaphysics, his religion, and his vision of man's ultimate development.

For the first of these specimen plays I have chosen *Major Barbara*. Published in 1907, it was one of the more stage-worthy of his comedies, and some of my older readers may remember the fine, successful New York performance by Grace George considerably more than a quarter of a century ago.

Man and Superman had been published some years before as the first of the synoptic versions of Shaw's philosophy. In *Major Barbara*, following what became something of a custom, he devotes a play to the further treatment of a theme briefly suggested before. In fact, *Major Barbara* might be thought of as simply a fable illustrating two sentences in

John Tanner's *Revolutionist's Handbook*. The first of these sentences is, "The only trouble with the poor is poverty." This I take to be about the simplest statement of Marxism that it would be possible to give. The second is an adjuration which sounds vaguely Nietzschian: "Beware of the man whose god is in the skies."

In the play, Barbara is the daughter of Andrew Undershaft, a successful and philosophical manufacturer of munitions. She leaves home because her father's business seems to her an evil one, and she joins the Salvation Army because it seems to be concerned directly with helping suffering humanity. Her father proposes a bargain. He will visit the Army shelter to see what she is accomplishing if she will then visit his factory. On the occasion of his visit, Barbara is disillusioned when the Army authorities accept a gift of "tainted money." When she goes to the factory, she is amazed by its orderly organization, by the work and good wages which it provides. Undershaft's employees are being more genuinely helped than the Salvation Army's recipients of a dole. Her father is curing poverty, not merely alleviating it. And you cannot see how much better this is if your god, like that of the Salvation Army, is in the skies. Apparently Barbara is converted from Christianity to Fabian socialism. Incidentally there is a young man, formerly a teacher of Greek, who beats the drum in the Salvation Army because this seems to him the most Dionysian activity possible in modern society.

It is significant that this plot, like all of Shaw's plots, even those of his most serious plays, is essentially farcical. That is another way of saying that it is at once perfectly logical and absolutely incredible. We do not for a moment believe that these events really happened. On the other hand, the rea-

sons why they never could have happened are reasons which
have to do not with logic, but with human psychology—
and human psychology is something with which Shaw never
bothers. He is never concerned with the way people do behave, but only with the way they would behave if they were
characters in a Shaw play.

We are, however, primarily concerned not with this fact,
but with the doctrine of the play. Shaw is, of course, not
defending the munitions industry as such. What he is saying
is simply that any industry, even this one, which provides
well-paid work under decent conditions is benefiting society. Undershaft is not primarily concerned with doing
good, but he is doing good whether he wants to or not. Moreover, as private industry becomes larger and more complicated, the simple profit motive of the owner becomes less
and less important as evolution in the direction of socialism
automatically takes place. Undershaft is simply one of the
links between capitalism and that socialism which is building itself. All that we need to do is to co-operate quietly
with the inevitable, and in a very short time the socialist
Utopia will have arrived as the result of—though he does
not use the term—dialectic materialism. No fable could
possibly set forth in simpler or more optimistic terms the
Fabian version of Marxism. And there are none of the conflicting ideas that I have mentioned earlier.

Translated into terms which we have been using in these
discussions, it might be put as follows. What the chasm
between the past and the future really separates is two systems for the organization of production. The bridge is being
quietly built for us, and almost before we know it we are
going to be on the other side, living in a Utopia where all
problems have been solved because the economic problem

has been solved. The only trouble with the poor is poverty, and soon there will be no more poverty.

Presently, however, even Shaw was compelled to admit that things were not working out that way. Instead of the peaceful dawn of socialism, what we had was the First World War, and *Heartbreak House*, one of the most interesting of all Shaw's plays, embodies his comment.

This time the central figure is not a vigorous, sanguine man cheerfully accomplishing a great work, but Captain Shotover, an aged sea captain who has retired from the world as well as from the sea and become one of those wise ancients whom Shaw was beginning to choose as his mouthpieces. He lives in a house built like a ship; he is surrounded by intelligent, irresponsible children and other relatives. This ship which is not going anywhere is obviously the ship of state; its inmates are the intelligent, feckless inhabitants of England.

They think that they live a charmed life. They are too clever and too amusing to suppose that anything unpleasant will ever happen to them. Nevertheless something very unpleasant is going to happen to them. One ominous warning appears in the form of a certain Boss Mangan, who intrudes somehow into the household and comes within an ace of buying with his money the most attractive granddaughter—partly because she has learned enough Shavianism to believe that poverty is the greatest evil and thinks that Boss Mangan would save her from poverty.

This Mangan is a capitalist; he owns stocks and he manipulates companies. But he is something very different from Andrew Undershaft of *Major Barbara*. Undershaft was a producer first and a capitalist second. Mangan is not a maker of anything except money. He is pure parasite. He never deals with anything more real than a stock certificate.

By the logic of *Major Barbara* he should never have come into existence. Undershaft should by now have turned into the manager of a state-owned industry. Somehow he has turned into a promoter instead. And a promoter is not a phenomenon of evolving socialism. The supposedly benign operations of the dialectic have not proved effective. Meanwhile, almost unnoticed, war clouds have been gathering. One evening while the whole company, talking brilliantly as usual, is in the garden, a first bomb falls out of the sky. Boss Mangan is killed, but miraculously, and for this once, no one else is hurt. In other words, the First World War is over. One result, so Shaw seems to say, is the death of the current version of capitalism. Nothing else useful, however, has been accomplished. Unless something is done, another bomb will fall someday. And one can hardly afford to trust to luck again.

Before the last curtain goes down, Captain Shotover gives the survivors a little lecture. In a sense, they have behaved very well. There was no panic, no cowardice. They did what had to be done for the moment. Englishmen are still cool-headed and brave. These are admirable qualities. But they are not going to be sufficient. The courage of Englishmen proves that they are worth saving. But it is not in itself sufficient to save them.

Looked at from another angle, *Heartbreak House* is a play which directly poses the question "What shall we do to be saved?" In *Major Barbara* the answer had seemed to be something like: "We don't have to do anything." Between the two plays, however, faith in inevitable social evolution has been discarded as Darwinism was to be. All the stress is now put upon conscious control. When Captain Shotover is asked the question directly, he replies in a seaman's terms: "Learn navigation." Learn, that is to say, the art of navigating the ship of state, the art of ruling and of being ruled.

No one in the play is ever more specific than that. But from this time on Shaw tended to become almost obsessed with the idea of rulers and the ruled. Before long he was publicly saying words in favor of the Fascists and the Communists. To his dying day he continued a sort of qualified defense of Stalin and Stalinism. Not, he was careful to say, that he approved of everything Communists did or everything they believed. Mechanism is nonsense. The great Soviet scientist Pavlov is pure idiot because he is pure mechanist. On the other hand, the Soviets have the right general idea. Men must be ruled; the ship of state has to be steered by a firm hand.

So far as we are concerned, the important point is simply that Shaw passes from bland optimism and cheerful reassurance to warnings of complete destruction—unless. After the First World War the chasm between the past and the future looks a great deal wider than it did. We shall cross it less soon and less easily than he had once thought. The chances are at least even that we shall not cross it at all, but shall fall into it instead. Moreover, what we will find on the other side, if we ever get there, is not what we had once supposed. It is not going to be the same, but better, world. It is going to be very different indeed.

Not so very many years ago, in one of his innumerable public utterances, Shaw remarked that he had recently received a letter from an American fundamentalist asking him why he did not abandon his nonsense and return to the Bible. "I replied," said Shaw, "by asking him which Bible he meant and whether he did not know that there were many Bibles." "Why," Shaw added, "I myself have written several." To the last and best of these Bibles we shall have to turn briefly for a final glimpse into the future as Shaw conceives it. The Bible in question is of course the five-part *Back to Methuselah*, which requires three evenings to play and which, to Shaw's own amazement, was actually produced in New York by the Theatre Guild in 1921. It begins in the Garden of Eden, and it ends many thousands of years hence in the most distant future which the imagination can reach. On the program it was subtitled *A Metabiological Pentateuch*. Though "metabiological" was not in the dictionaries, its meaning is plain. If metaphysics is what comes after physics, metabiology must be what comes after biology—it must be, therefore, the ultimate philosophical conclusions which can be reached if one starts out from our knowledge, not of the laws of the physical world, but of what we know of the laws of living organisms. It ought to include very nearly everything, and *Back to Methuselah* does. It is Shaw's most inclusive prophecy.

Fortunately it is not necessary for our purposes to examine all the details of this apocalyptic vision. As a matter of fact, the apparently innocent whimsey suggested by the title is sufficient. As anyone who has ever read or seen the play is almost certain to remember, this title refers to an event which takes place near the middle—at a period supposed to represent a time just a little in advance of our own. Human society has got into a rather bad way. In fact, the general state of affairs is much like that in *Heartbreak House* and the same question arises: "What shall we do to save ourselves?" A small group of unusually able people realizes that the only possible answer is a very radical one. Man as he now exists is simply not competent to manage the terribly complex affairs of the world. The most obvious reason is that he does not live long enough, not long enough to learn the things which he ought to know. The obvious solution is to live longer, and that is what a select group of people begin to do. They live for three or four hundred years, and during the last couple of centuries of their lives they are competent managers of the world's affairs.

I have called this a whimsey, and it may seem unreasonable to base a serious criticism on a whimsey. One may also say that Shaw's invoking of a miraculous increase in the human life span as a bridge between the past and the future is only a manner of speaking, only a rather moderate way of phrasing Nietzsche's saying, "Man is something which must be surpassed." Whatever you call it, whimsey, or manner of speaking, it involves a staggering admission on the part of one who had previously represented himself as an optimist. To the question "How can man be saved?" he now gives the answer "Only a miracle can save him"; and no amount of whimsicality can disguise the fact that this is what *Back to Methuselah* does say.

Moreover, once the miracle is assumed to have taken place, human society and human nature proceed along a path of evolution which renders both unrecognizable by, and rather dubiously attractive to, those of us who are still dominated by old-fashioned human nature and rather doubtful about our desire to be quite so drastically changed. The outlines of the Utopia which Shaw imagines our reaching are as dim as those of the old-fashioned nonconformist heaven and inevitably seem to many almost as dull. About all we are told is that art, love, and social intercourse are confined to the infants who have been hatched out of eggs at what we would call an adolescent age. The mature citizens are Ancients with long beards who smile at the young with kindly condescension and spend their time in ecstatic contemplation. We shall not reach this society for many thousands of years, and we seem destined to a lot of troubles between then and now. John Tanner had said, "Beware of the man whose god is in the skies." Might he not now say to his creator, "Beware the man whose heaven is in the unimaginably distant future."

Before we reach the last of this series of discussions, something will have to be said to demonstrate that Shaw does mean quite seriously and almost literally what *Back to Methuselah* whimsically presents: that only through a miracle—and a miracle not very likely to happen—can man be saved. For the time being we shall merely sum up what has been the thesis of this very limited discussion of one special aspect of Shaw's plays, the aspect under which they are seen when they are considered simply as his contribution to the presentation in dramatic form of certain aspects of the chasm between the past and the future.

My thesis is that, despite his delightful, his irresistible comic gifts and despite what was originally a determined optimism born of a naturally sanguine temperament, Shaw's ultimate conclusions are in important respects considerably less different from those of other less outwardly cheerful "modern" dramatists than one would have expected. The longer he considers it, the wider and deeper the chasm between the past and the future appears to be and the greater is the difficulty of getting across it.

We chose to consider the changes in his attitude as revealed in three successive plays written over a period of about a quarter of a century and spanning his most productive period. In the first, *Major Barbara*, we are told that we seem destined to reach peaceably, rather soon, and without any great effort on our part a happy society which is simply our own with all the difficulties and injustices removed. In *Heartbreak House* the difficulties and dangers have been greatly increased. The Marxian dialectic is no longer going to solve our problems for us. We shall have to learn the difficult art of navigation. Finally, when we get to *Back to Methuselah*, we discover an even greater difficulty. The necessary art of navigation is beyond our capacity to learn. Man as we know him is not smart enough to save himself. He will have to learn to live three or four hundred years or in some other way become much more intelligent and competent than he now is. Admittedly this is going to take many thousands of years at best. When and if it really does happen, neither man nor his society will be anything which we could possibly understand or have much interest in. Thus Shaw's "optimism" turns out to be more a matter of temperament than of philosophical conviction. The chief difference between him and the more usual despairing modern is simply this: Shaw takes his despair more cheerfully. He wears his rue with a difference.

4 / Pirandello and the Dissolution of the Ego

THUS far I have attempted to demonstrate that the "modernism" so ardently hailed by Ibsen ultimately revealed itself as a series of dilemmas to each of the four playwrights whom we have considered. It seemed to bring them, not to a solution of the problems of the good life and the good society, but to an impasse.

I have not and do not intend to argue the question of the extent to which the thought of these dramatists was original with them or even of the extent to which they rather than philosophers or novelists or sociologists made the most effective propaganda for it. I have merely taken it for granted that we could analyze the thought in their plays and that my readers would recognize the close relationship between certain aspects of "modernism" in the drama and "modernism" as we meet it elsewhere.

In the two final essays I shall discuss more recent playwrights and ask whether or not one may find in any of them hints at least of a reaction against modernism and a reaffirmation of certain important things denied by the kind of modernists we have been discussing. One or two of them, it seems to me, refuse to believe that the past and the future are as nearly discontinuous as a Shaw or an Ibsen would suggest; they seem to assume that modern man is not fundamentally different from man as he has been and that the society of the future will not be totally unlike the society of the past. After all, most of the modernists began by promising us a better world which, by now, we seem unlikely to reach along their road.

This eventual change of direction is mentioned at this point in order to offset somewhat the negative tone which I have so far been compelled to take and which, unfortunately, I shall have to continue for a little longer. There still remain two or three other famous playwrights each of whom in his own individual way both widens the chasm between the past and the future and, like the others, seems in the end to show us how to fall into it rather than how to get across.

Most people would probably agree that Ibsen, Strindberg, Shaw, and perhaps Wilde were key figures in the intellectually ambitious drama of the late nineteenth and early twentieth centuries. But if one is to choose two or three others the choice is less obvious.

Without undertaking any elaborate defense of my choice, I shall pick the Russian Anton Chekhov and the Italian Pirandello, remarking only that both are widely read as well as occasionally performed today and that they are often spoken of with respect by the younger generation of literary critics which seems to find little of interest in Ibsen and Shaw. Both are, in many respects, very different in method and mood from the writers whom we have so far discussed. This makes all the more significant the fact that both of them nevertheless also reach an impasse which, as I have been suggesting, seems to be the thing that all the significant dramatists of the period had in common.

Obviously Chekhov is as much "Russian" as he is "modern." Before him Turgenev, Tolstoi, and Dostoevski had already made Russian literature part of world literature. Thanks to them every literate person in Europe had heard about the remarkable "Russian soul," with its passion, its mysticism, and its violence. The English-speaking world which had been brought up on decorous domestic novelists from Samuel Richardson through Jane Austen to Thackeray and Trollope was amazed to discover that life could be lived on a different level, and the great issues become not propriety, but sin and religious ecstasy. Tolstoi's all-or-nothing demand for righteousness rather than for mere decency and Dostoevski's Christian version of the Dionysian instance that life is good because it is painful came to the Anglo-Saxon world as a new revelation of the excitement possible in the novel.

Chekhov belonged to the age which followed the heroic generation of Tolstoi and Dostoevski. At times his characters live, or think that they live, in the world of his predecessors. One is tempted to say that they all seem to have read Tolstoi and Dostoevski and are trying to be Tolstoi and Dostoevski characters. But Chekhov has lost the passion of his predecessors because he has lost the faith which sustains it. He and often his characters are skeptics rather than believers. The soul searchings of his personages are not terrible but, frequently, ridiculous, and it is their futility rather than their tragedy which most impresses him. Whereas Tolstoi and Dostoevski were prophets, he is a critic and a satirist. They believed; he doubts. They saw tragedy; he sees, at most, pathos, usually tinged with absurdity.

Chekhov was, of course, well known as a short-story writer before he tried the theater. He would have been an important literary figure if the modern drama had never existed. It was, nevertheless, the foundation in Moscow of a theater consciously devoted to the "new" theatrical activity that led to his development as a dramatist and ultimately made his plays as well known as his stories. *The Sea Gull* had been first produced at the Imperial Russian Theater, where it proved so complete a failure that Chekhov vowed never to write another play. A few years later it was revived with great success at the "advanced" Moscow Art Theater and achieved the success which established it as a standard item in the repertory, where it remained for many years and even survived the Bolshevist revolution.

It is no accident that the title of *The Sea Gull* suggests at once *The Wild Duck*. Ibsen's "symbolism," his use of usually somewhat ambiguous objects or incidents to suggest a rather vague allegory, was one of the features of his style often imitated, as it was in France especially, by writers not particularly sympathetic to his sociological and realistic elements. The extent to which Chekhov was influenced is shown again in *The Cherry Orchard*, where the orchard symbolizes the grace and beauty of the past which is being sacrificed because it has no utilitarian value.

If the whole rather awkward business about the dead bird as a symbol of dead happiness is somewhat perfunctory and self-conscious Ibsen, most of the play is pure Chekhov, and nothing is more strikingly so than the two opening lines of the dialogue. The curtain goes up on two middle-aged people doing nothing on a country estate. "Why," asks the man, "do you always wear black?" And the woman replies, "I am in mourning for my dead life."

It is possible to play this opening scene and indeed the whole play with unrelieved solemnity. It has sometimes been so played in the United States. It would, however, also be possible to play it as well as various other scenes as pure farce. Chekhov's own remarks, especially in his letters, indicate that he himself was more aware of the comic aspect of his plays than were the Russian interpreters upon occasion. Yet *The Sea Gull* does end with a suicide; nearly everybody in it is miserable; and it can hardly be interpreted as though it were intended to be merely funny. Actually, it is both funny and sad, the chief characters both pathetic and ridiculous. They perpetually dramatize themselves and especially their unhappiness. They talk endlessly about Life with a capital L, about Love, about the Beautiful, and about all the other great abstractions which Anglo-Saxons are generally ashamed to mention. They see themselves and their fate as grandiose, but they are, in fact, never passionate enough to achieve Tolstoian or Dostoevskian dimensions, and their fates generally creep gradually upon them. They are hardly tragic. One can say only that they are pathetically ridiculous. Melancholy has marked them for her own. Almost from childhood they have known that they would be unhappy, and the most they generally hope for is that their unhappiness will be of a kind which others will recognize as an interesting unhappiness. They do have charm—a word we have never used in connection with Ibsen or Strindberg or Shaw—and so do the plays in which they figure. But the whole tone is elegiac and resigned.

Though it is clear that Chekhov often laughs at his characters, he nevertheless holds them in great affection. Perhaps he recognizes in their quiet bafflement something of himself. Undoubtedly he sees them as typical of something characteristic of his race and his time. But why are they like this? Offhand we may be inclined to answer, "Because they are Russians; this is what we have been told the Russian soul is like." Chekhov himself suggests a somewhat different answer.

They are, of course, recognizably "Russian," but the Russian soul had not always manifested itself in so passive and resigned a form. Moreover, the answer which Chekhov seems to give suggests immediately a connection with the theme of our discussion. The real trouble with these people is that they belong to the past. They are the surviving nobility and gentry of a dead age. They do nothing because there is nothing for them to do. Their political, social, and economic environment has disappeared, leaving them stranded. They are lost between two worlds, one dead, the other powerless to be born.

Now and then one of them expresses his realization of this fact in political or sociological terms. His futility takes the form of a futile idealism directed toward "the future." A great new day will dawn, he thinks. The world will be ruled by justice, and all men will be happy and prosperous. Our great-great-great-grandchildren will look back at us with pity and wonder.

In so far as Chekhov was political at all, he himself was a liberal. His plays were regarded by the Czarist government as mildly dangerous, and with that curious, hesitant repressiveness characteristic of it the authorities did put certain restrictions on the presentation of his plays without forbidding them entirely. Actually, of course, Chekhov was not very political, and it would be more unqualifiedly true to say of him than even of Ibsen that he was more a poet than a social philosopher. What absorbed him was not the future but the present. He was more interested in what the characters in his plays were like than in the question why they were like that.

It has become one of the characteristics of our own time that when we find ourselves faced with any phenomenon, whether it be an animal, a social institution, or even a work of art, we immediately ask two questions: "What were its origins? What will be its future development?" Our interest in these questions concerning evolution and ultimate destiny have become so obsessive that we seldom bother to ask what a thing *is*—now and in itself. Possibly that is one result of a conviction that, being in transition, we have no significant present. But one of the reasons why Chekhov's plays have seemed so fascinating to so many is that they are, curiously, concerned primarily with what a special group of people is like rather than with how they got that way or what will become of them. Perhaps a thing can be loved only when it is thus accepted in its own terms, and perhaps the fact that Chekhov loved his characters is an important part of his uniqueness.

Nevertheless it is because he too was aware to some extent of the two abstractions, the Past and the Future, that he is relevant to our discussion and that he can give us as he does a glimpse at the problem from an angle somewhat different from any we have so far been afforded. If he had been simply unconcerned with the future and engaged in nothing but a defense of his dying aristocrat, he would merely have been a possibly interesting conservative and would not have come into our discussion at all. If, on the contrary, he had been, as the early Soviet critics tried to make him, a sort of John the Baptist of the Revolution preparing the way for the appearance of Lenin, he would be almost equally irrelevant. What he does exhibit is one of the characteristic features of what I have been calling modernism in the drama. He too ends with a dilemma.

The play which most directly and clearly illustrates this fact is *The Cherry Orchard*, where the situation is simplicity itself. A group of typically feckless and typically charming Chekhovian gentry are losing their estate to an up-and-coming Man of the Future. His first act is to lay an ax to their cherry orchard in order to make way for a more economic use of the land, and "Is this good or bad?" is the only question posed in the play. Characteristically, the aesthetic effect of the play does not depend upon any answers being given. Chekhov's tone is as usual elegiac, rather than philosophical or polemic. The one indisputable thing upon which the emotional attention centers is the fact that something beautiful is being destroyed—the useless cherry orchard itself and the useless lives of the people whom it symbolized. This destruction is in itself sad and pitiful whether one resents it as an evil or accepts it as something necessary and, in the end, productive of good.

Though the play is thus not primarily a problem play, both Chekhov himself and some of the characters recognize the problem implicit. One character in particular philosophizes the incidents and talks glowingly of the future, although one realizes that his talk, like that of nearly all Chekhov's characters, will never be anything but talk.

Plainly Chekhov's own answer to the question posed is simply that no clear-cut answer is possible. The thing is both good and bad. No doubt it had to happen. But the present loss is at least as certain as any future gain. Whatever may be said in favor of the new world, one thing seems clear. There will be no place for Cherry Trees in it, at least for a long time to come. One cannot stand up against the Future. But one cannot be too happy about it either.

This is the dilemma in Chekhov, and I might add that the gentleness with which it is stated makes it a peculiarly Chekhovian manifestation of the tendency in modernism to reach such a dilemma. There is another reason why this particular play should be mentioned now. This is the first time that we have met the admission that the past is not merely something to grow away from, that something in itself worth having may be left behind when and if we cross the chasm. Nostalgia for the past is the very last thing one would expect to find in either Shaw or Ibsen. It is a very strong element in Chekhov.

One of the factors contributing to his purely artistic originality and effectiveness is the peculiar dramatic form, the method of storytelling, which he developed in order to produce the effect intended and which one is tempted to call the method of the dramatically undramatic. Because of it a common complaint of his characters is that nothing ever happens to them, that life has passed them by; in a word, that their existence is without drama. To some extent this is true; to some extent on the other hand, it is a delusion cultivated as all their delusions are cultivated in order to make them seem pathetic to themselves. And if their creator is to make us share their mood, he must make us also feel that nothing is happening. That obviously creates a problem for the dramatist whose audience is going to expect that a good deal should happen in a play.

This problem Chekhov solved so successfully that, though something always does happen, critics as well as lay spectators often declare that nothing does, and the static character of his plays becomes a standing joke. Of the play *The Three Sisters* it has been said that the plot might be summarized as follows. In the first act three sisters living in the provinces wish that they could go to Moscow but are unable to do so. In the second act they again wish that they could go to Moscow and again do not do so. In the third act they still wish that they could go to Moscow and they still do not go.

If one depends upon a general impression, it may seem that not much more actually happens in *The Sea Gull*. Yet, as a matter of fact, the action of the story told in that play includes among other things a seduction and a suicide— two events much relied upon by playwrights in search of something undeniably dramatic. The most obvious reason why Chekhov can keep them from seeming so is that they both take place off stage, and in general Chekhov tends to communicate to the spectators the characters' own conviction that their lives are eventless by exhibiting them during the eventless moments of their career.

In the mid-nineteenth century the exponents of what was termed "the well-made play" talked about what they called "the obligatory scene." Within certain limits the playwright, they said, is free to choose what parts of an action he will actually exhibit on the stage. In every story, however, there are crucial moments which the dramatist simply cannot refuse to face and which are "obligatory" in the sense that an audience will rightfully demand to see them happening before its eyes. The simplest description of Chekhov's method would be that he nearly always omits the obligatory scene which nearly always takes place either off stage or, like the seduction just referred to, between the acts and while the audience is chatting in the lobby. One agrees with the characters that nothing ever happens to them because one never sees it happen.

One specific illustration of how the matter is handled will suffice. *The Sea Gull*, you will remember, opens with the bit about the lady who is mourning for her dead life. Let us see how the play ends. A character enters in some agitation and whispers to another: "Don't say anything about it now, but the fact is that Constantine has shot himself." Curtain.

Let us compare that with another famous stage suicide. Othello, the Moor, has decided that he no longer wants to live or deserves to do so. But he makes a speech of some nineteen lines, first reviewing his career and then analyzing his character.

> I have done the state some service, and they know't—
> No more of that. I pray you, in your letters,
> When you shall these unlucky deeds relate,
> Speak of me as I am. Nothing extenuate,
> Nor set down aught in malice. Then must you speak
> Of one that lov'd not wisely, but too well;
> Of one not easily jealous but, being wrought,
> Perplex'd in the extreme . . .

Finally, dramatizing his own drama:

> And say besides that in Aleppo once,
> Where a malignant and a turban'd Turk
> Beat a Venetian and traduc'd the state,
> I took by th' throat the circumcised dog
> And smote him—thus.

Stage direction: "Stabs himself and dies."

That is a method very different from Chekhov's. Can you imagine Shakespeare throwing away an opportunity like this? Can you imagine him ending *Othello* by having one character whisper to another, "Don't say anything about it now, but the fact is that Othello has killed himself"? For him the obligatory scene really was obligatory.

If I discuss this matter here, it is not merely for the sake of whatever purely technical interest it may have but because of something which the choice of method seems to reveal about Chekhov's relation to the mood of the other "modern" dramatists whom we have been considering. Shakespeare presents the great passionate moments on the stage because he and his audience believe that in them the true meaning of life is revealed and the most noteworthy aspects of human experience exhibited. Chekhov avoids them because he seems to share, and expect his audience to share, the awareness of his characters that the most characteristic aspect of life is that under which it presents itself as a flat, melancholy, and featureless plain. It is this, of course, which serves to justify his plaintive and nostalgic tone.

Neither Ibsen, nor Strindberg, nor Wilde, nor Shaw commonly exhibits anything resembling this Chekhovian resignation. Even in the face of what I have called his pessimistic implications, Shaw persists in proclaiming a sort of jaunty optimism. As an aesthete, Wilde believes in splendor and hopes for pleasure if not for happiness. Ibsen insists with a sort of somber optimism that something can be done about it. Even Strindberg responds to unresolvable conflict, not with resignation, but with Dionysian fury. Perhaps, as I suggested before, there is some connection between the various aspects of Chekhov's uniqueness. Perhaps both the elegiac tone and the curiously undramatic dramatic method are both the result of the fact that he has not wholly committed himself to the future or willingly surrendered all of the past. He acknowledges, as none of the others do, a sense of loss, and instead of concerning himself exclusively with what the world is going to become, he looks back, sometimes longingly, towards what it once was.

The objection may be raised that I have persistently defined my dramatists in terms of what they deny rather than of what they affirm. Ibsen denies the existence of absolutes. Strindberg denies the possibility of reconciling conflicting impulses. Shaw denies that man as he exists is capable of solving his problems. Now Chekhov denies, among other things, the significance of the drama.

Perhaps this objection would be valid if I were pretending to give a complete account. I say only "perhaps" because part of my thesis is that the playwrights whom we have been discussing actually deny more and affirm less than is commonly supposed. In any event my procedure is both inevitable and necessary in view of my special purpose, and I shall apply it still more narrowly in the discussion of the last of my negative dramatists, the Italian Luigi Pirandello. Pirandello's plays have been variously interpreted, and a well-known contemporary critic has recently assigned him a very high place in the modern drama. Without questioning that judgment I shall treat him exclusively, from the point of view of my thesis, as the dramatist who has made—or, as perhaps it would be safer to say of so ambiguous a dramatist, seems to me to have made—the most inclusive denial of all, namely, the denial that the persistent and more or less consistent character or personality which we attribute to each individual human being, and especially to ourselves, really exists at all.

This is perhaps the most elusive subject which I shall have to discuss, partly because the assumption that "I am I" and that "You are You" is one of the most fundamental which we make—because it seems self-evident to us, not only that the realities exist but also that they persist, so that the "I" of today and the "I" of yesterday are in some way continuous no matter what developments may occur. Upon this assumption all moral systems must rest, since obviously no one can be good or bad, guilty or innocent, unless he exists as some sort of continuous unity. Ultimately, not only all moral systems but all other attempts to deal systematically with the phenomena of human life depend upon it. Even the mechanists who deny free will and insist that an individual personality or character is merely the product of the conditioning influences which have come to bear upon it need nevertheless to assume that this externally determined character is some sort of persistent entity. For the mechanist too, the "I" must at least exist.

If Pirandello were a completely isolated phenomenon or even if similar attitudes had been exhibited only in the drama, he would be too aberrant a phenomenon to find a place in the present discussion. In his case, however, as in the case of all the other playwrights whom we have considered, the dramatist represents attitudes which appear in other writers and which he took, not necessarily from these other writers, but perhaps out of the air—as Ibsen said he got his ideas. So conspicuously is this true that what I am about to discuss, namely the phenomenon which has been called "the dissolution of the ego," has sometimes been described as one of the most significant processes in modern thought.

I do not mean to deny that a certain paradox in the

common-sense concept of the "I" has not been recognized for a very long time. After all, Heraclitus maintained that nothing persisted except change, and an ancient Greek joke turns upon the case of the wrongdoer who protests that he should not be punished today for what "he" did yesterday, since no "he" has really persisted from one day into the next. Despite the occasional toying with such paradoxes, Greek ethics no less than Christian ethics depend upon the assumption that separate and internally continuous personalities do exist.

We know that men are often inconsistent, but it would not mean anything to say that they are inconsistent if we did not assume that there is something consistent with which they are temporarily inconsistent. We say of a man's action that it was "unlike him" to do this or that. We solemnly adjure him to be "true to himself," or we flippantly advise him, "Be yourself!" The recognition of an inconsistency implies a prior and more significant recognition of a consistency. You cannot be true to yourself unless there is a self to whom you can be true.

I have just said that all classical and all Christian ethics assume this persistent, continuous reality of the ego and could not exist without it. I might add that without it history and storytelling also would be, in any ordinary form of either, likewise impossible, since a narrative moving through time implies something, namely man, recognizably continuous which moves with the narrative and through it. Yet in Pirandello we have the case of a playwright who does attempt to write some sort of drama while seeming to deny this generally indispensable assumption. After a very brief illustration of what I mean by this, I shall say a few words about the parallel between this odd enterprise and certain other literary phenomena of recent days. First let us take for discussion one play by Pirandello.

He is the author of several, more or less well known, and they exhibit a strong family resemblance to one another. However, in this country at least, the best known is *Six Characters in Search of an Author*, which had a successful Broadway run almost a generation ago in a fine production with Florence Eldridge as star.

In *Six Characters* the curtain goes up on the stage of a theater occupied by a director who is considering a new production. Six persons force their way in, declare that they are characters created by a playwright who abandoned them, and insist upon their right to act out the events they were created to act. Against the manager's protests they take over the stage and do enact a sordid and complicated story about the relations of a man with the wife from whom he is separated and with her children by him and by a lover. Everyone in the play is tortured by jealousy, love, hatred, and, above all perhaps, by a sense of shame.

Without the peculiar setting of play within play and without all the metaphysical embellishments, what we should have is a rather lurid tragic melodrama. But we are obviously intended to be primarily interested, not in this story as a story, but in what the author uses it to say about the nature of reality. Psychological dramas are common. *Six Characters in Search of an Author* is not so much psychological as it is metaphysical.

The skepticism to which it would persuade us is almost all-inclusive. The thesis seems to be that the human being cannot distinguish between appearance and reality—even, perhaps, that no such distinction exists. Reality is merely that appearance in which I happen to believe, merely that form of insanity of which I happen to be the victim. Or to quote the title of another Pirandello play: "Right You Are If You Think You Are."

Thus at the very beginning the distinction between "real life" and make-believe is broken down when the six characters enter the world of "real life" and begin to operate on the same plane as that of the theatrical manager. Art, it seems, is no less real than nature. Perhaps it is even more real because the imagined character exists in eternity, the living man only temporarily in time, and also, perhaps, because a character in fiction may be given a consistent ego which a character in real life does not have.

Moreover, even within the framework of the play within a play, everything is almost equally dubious. The various characters see the various events, and especially they see one another, in various lights. The playwright remains neutral. One character is not right, or sane, or logical, and the others somehow wrong. There is no assumed version of things "as they really are" because no one, not even the playwright, could know what that version is even if it exists.

Inevitably the most dubious and elusive in the midst of all this dubiety are the characters, personalities, and motives of the dramatis personae. Every individual has many "I's." He is, of course, what he seems to himself, but he is also all the things which he seems to all the different people who know him. And there is no guarantee that his version of himself is any truer than any one of the others.

Merely as a passing fancy this sort of Pyrrhic skepticism is no doubt as old as critical thought. From its paralyzing effect we are ordinarily saved by what Santayana calls "animal faith." We admit that life may be only a dream and that we may know nothing outside the fancies of our own brains, but the animal faith which bids us believe in the external world is much stronger than any metaphysical arguments. Everybody acts as though he believed that the external world exists; nearly everybody acts as though he believed that his version of it is a dependable one; and the majority act as though they could also make valid value judgments about it. Not merely in one play, but in a whole series of plays, Pirandello carries on an attack against our animal faith and seems determined to persuade us not merely that we cannot make value judgments, not merely that we cannot distinguish appearance from reality, but that the whole concept of reality as opposed to appearance is inadmissible.

Moreover and in the process, the "I" itself, the thing which perceives appearances and becomes the victim of illusions, disintegrates—if, at least, one means by the "I" any continuous, persisting, relatively stable thing. Every "I" is not merely all the things which at various times it seems to itself to be or all the things which at various times it seems to various people to be. It is also all the different things which at different times it has been. There are the "I's" of yesterday, today, and tomorrow, as well as what every observer has taken each of them to be. At one point in the play the husband, who has been caught in a ridiculous and even, in his judgment, a reprehensible act, protests against being judged by it; protests, that is, against the assumption that this action is typical of him or that, as we should say, he is "that kind of man." But from the standpoint of the play this is, of course, absurd. It assumes that he has a character as distinguished from the sum of all the inconsistent things which he does, that he is "being himself" at certain moments and not "being himself" at others. What, Pirandello seems to ask, can a "self" be except what it is being from moment to moment?

I have already remarked that the tendency which Pirandello carries to a logical or illogical extreme is not unique in him and that, as a matter of fact, this tendency to "dissolve the ego" has been sometimes regarded as one highly characteristic of our times. No doubt the direction taken by much psychological investigation has a good deal to do with the tendency. This investigation has tended to pay particular attention to "states of mind" rather than to what is loosely called "character." It has made us very much aware of inconsistencies and illogicalities in our feeling and conduct, of conflicts and opposing impulses. As a result we tend to think of others and sometimes of ourselves not in terms of a hard core of character occasionally obscured by "uncharacteristic" attitudes but as being simply, from moment to moment, the temporary resultant of the various forces being brought to bear at that moment upon our consciousness and our unconsciousness.

The Christian, and to an almost equal extent the classic, conception of the "persona" or of the "ego" seems to have been of a fully conscious unity, of a soul captain, born with us at birth and perhaps created by God. It is an ultimate, even *the* ultimate continuous reality persisting through time. This ego may develop itself or it may corrupt itself, but it can never cease to *be* itself. To its integrity and to its will we may appeal, and we may, more or less sternly, hold it to some extent accountable for what it does.

Inevitably the tendencies of modern psychology at least modify somewhat this classical conception of the "I." If we accept the theory of the unconscious and its role, if we assume that the "I" is a sort of iceberg at least three-fifths below the water line of awareness, then the "I" must become at least a double rather than a single thing. Whether or not the concepts of modern psychology, even assuming that they are entirely correct, really necessarily lead to the complete dissolution of the "I" is another question. I have no intention of opening it directly here; I have only the intention of suggesting that this tendency to dissolve it is characteristic and that, if I may return once more to the central metaphor, one of the most significant differences between the past which lies on one side of a chasm and the future which is presumed to lie on the other is simply that the past is dominated by egos, by actors who are assumed to be directed by a hard-core personality, while in the future there will be only states of consciousness—continuous only in the sense that they function for a time by means of a given brain, housed in a given skull.

Earlier I said that I wanted to say something about other manifestations in recent literature of the dissolving ego. I shall note only two things, first, that the whole "stream of consciousness" method tends to stress the fluid as opposed to the hard-core aspect of the individual personality even when there is no dogmatic assertion that the stream is either the only or the most significant aspect of the personality. Secondly, let me say that Marcel Proust's *Remembrance of Things Past* is both one of the most impressive works of modern literature and one in which the "dissolution of the ego" is most conspicuous. This dissolution was a theme of which the author himself was fully conscious and one to which he returned again and again. Swann, the Duchesse de Guermantes, and Monsieur de Charlus persist as names. But much of the book depends upon Proust's own sense that the personalities bearing these names are not at any moment what they were at any previous time and that the conception which he first formed when he heard about them is much more enduringly real than the manifestations in the flesh which from time to time he encounters. No doubt Pirandello was influenced, as Proust was, by Bergson's insistence that the ultimate reality is change in time. Whatever the reason, Proust's denial of the classical ego is only less fanatically stated, not much less thoroughgoing in fact, than Pirandello's.

It is a curious fact that the three most revolutionary new hypotheses of the nineteenth century—Darwinism, Marxism, and Freudism—should have had one thing and one thing only in common. All three are, or at least were popularly taken to be, hypotheses which tended to take man's fate out of his own hands, to assure him that he could not do the supremely important things for himself, and then to tell him also, by way of compensation, that he therefore could not be blamed for anything which happened to him.

According to Darwinism, the evolution from lower to higher is in the hands of an automatic process called natural selection. According to Marx, the development of social justice is in the hands of an automatic process called dialectical materialism. According to Freud—or at least according to Freud's popular interpreters—the character and the conduct of the individual depends, not upon his own free choice, but upon the experiences, traumatic or otherwise, to which he has been exposed and especially to those which he underwent in infancy. All three of these hypotheses lend themselves to what I should call philosophies of exculpation. Each is discouraging in the sense that it denies us the power radically to control our destiny, soothing in the sense that it assures us we are at least not to blame.

About each of these hypotheses I had said something before we came to the dissolution of the ego with which we are at present concerned. Unfortunately this last cannot be reduced to terms as simple as the others, and on the part of the general public there is not so acute a realization of it. The average literate man knows that he accepts or rejects what he thinks of as Darwinism, Marxism, or Freudism; but he is much less likely to be aware of the extent to which he has lost the classical sense of the "I" as an ultimate, persistent, unified thing whose continuous existence is the most self-evident of realities and without which the whole world of his mental and physical awareness would be a meaningless flux. Yet in so far as he has, even without knowing it, lost that sense he has undergone a very fateful change. Few things could cut him off more completely from any understanding of or participation in a past which did think of the universe as inhabited by "I's."

No doubt Darwinism, Marxism, and Freudism all contributed to the dissolution of the ego. The sense that we are directing our destiny is one of the things which convinces us that our "I" is real, and anything which casts doubt upon the power of self-direction weakens our belief in the reality of the ego. But I have chosen to discuss the dissolution of the ego as a separate topic, not merely because Pirandello and Proust afford us striking examples in contemporary literature of the artist's concern with the phenomenon, but also because it is something more than an obvious and predictable result of Darwin and Marx and Freud. It is one thing to say: "I am not a free agent. What I am and what I do is the result of natural selection, of the dialectic of the material universe, and of the psychic traumas of my infancy." Another step must be taken before one can add that the "I" is not only not self-determining but that it does not, in any easily understandable sense, exist at all except as a perpetually shifting configuration.

From any attempt even to suggest the major consequences for society, philosophy, religion, and morals of a general and complete renunciation of the classical concept of the ego, I retire appalled. I shall simply leave them to your imagination and conclude with a consideration comically less portentous. What would be the effect upon the drama if the theories and the procedure of both Chekhov and Pirandello were universally adopted by playwrights and carried to their logical conclusions?

Theorists have generally maintained that the soul of the drama is either action or character. Aristotle seems to maintain the supremacy of the first when he declares that "the fable" is the most important part of a tragedy. Many moderns, on the other hand, have insisted that the revelation of character through conflict is more important than story. Offhand I cannot think of any analyst who has maintained that you could have a play without either action on the one hand or the revelation of character on the other. Yet Chekhov gets rid of action and Pirandello gets rid of character. One is tempted to suggest somewhat light-mindedly that whatever else we may or may not be able to predict about the future which lies across the chasm one thing seems fairly certain: There will not be any plays in it.

5 / Synge and the Irish Protest

PERHAPS I should, at this point, ask myself the question which many of my readers have no doubt been asking. Is this account which I have given of certain aspects of the modern drama really sober rather than fanatical or fantastic? Have I been determined to find sinister, destructive implications, and have I overinterpreted as well as over-emphasized whatever I could find?

I have already admitted that I am not professing to tell the whole truth and that I have been primarily interested in what do seem to me sinister implications. Granted that admission, I am prepared to insist that I have invented nothing and that what I have attempted to expose is really there.

Ibsen did deny that any truth is permanent or absolute. Strindberg did assert that the conflicts within human nature are unresolvable. Shaw does maintain that man, both as he is and as for a long time he is likely to be, cannot solve his problems because he is not intelligent or virtuous enough to do so. Pirandello does imply both that appearance is indistinguishable from reality and that if we fall back upon any determination to be "true to ourselves," to take refuge in the integrity of our own ego, we are putting our faith in something which does not exist.

Soberly to acquiesce in any one of these negations is to surrender a premise upon which most men at most times have relied. To acquiesce in all of them is to enter a new and bewildering world which has lost almost completely its familiar shape.

I use the phrase "soberly to acquiesce" because I recognize that there are many levels of belief and that most of the time there are in our minds many beliefs which we neither wholly accept nor wholly reject. For one thing, probably no man not certifiably insane ever totally divests himself of animal faith, so that if, for example, he professes absolute determinism, he also always acts as though he could by an exercise of his will affect to some extent his destiny. At moments most of us believe or believe that we believe what at other moments we do not act upon. It is impossible, therefore, to say precisely to what extent the logical consequences of the denial of absolutes, or the sense that the classical ego has been dissolved, has influenced the practical world and increased our difficulties in dealing with it or even contributed significantly to that sense of disillusion, of anxiety, and of pessimism which is commonly said to be characteristic of our age. But that the disturbing ideas which we have been analyzing out of certain highly esteemed modern plays have had some influence upon all these things seems to me a safe enough assertion.

In the early days modernism was commonly supposed by its proponents to promise a better world in the rather proximate future. Very few people today believe that a radically better world is close at hand. As a matter of fact, what one hears most often discussed nowadays is not Utopia but quite boldly the possibility of survival. Certain of the ideas which we have been considering are obvious concomitants of this change from hope to desperation.

What I have been doing, what I announced from the beginning that I would do, is simply to trace in certain modern plays certain tendencies which seem to me to have contributed to the creation of an impossible mental environment. It is not that I am insisting or even suggesting that these plays were supremely important as an influence, though they no doubt had a ponderable one. The significant fact is that the same tendencies could be found in almost any department of mental activity which one should choose to examine. Perhaps the case will be strongest if I go only so far as to say, "Even in the drama the chasm was widening between the past and the future—if there is any future in which creatures like us can participate."

Having said this, I shall consider that I have concluded what I have to say about my principal thesis, or at least about the first section of it. The plays upon which I have based it belong to a recent past which is, nevertheless, definitely a past and to a generation now no longer young. A new generation has meanwhile grown up. Since nearly everything I have said about the older one was intended to make it sound ominous, the inevitable question which remains is this: "What of the plays and the playwrights who have more recently attracted serious attention? Is there any sign in the drama of attitudes effectively opposed to these we have been considering, anything which might serve to re-establish the credit of the key concepts that had been under persistent attack? Is the immediate future in literature in general and in the drama in particular likely to be merely the immediate past all over again?"

I need hardly remind you that in literary criticism a very effective group has been busy stressing the importance of the continuity of tradition rather than the reality of the chasm between the past and the future. Its leader, T. S. Eliot, happens also to be extremely conservative in religious, political, and social opinions. But the relation of many who have followed his aesthetic lead to the whole body of his opinions is often very complex because many of those who have, for example, written verse in imitation of his manner have been radicals of various sorts rather than conservatives. Without going into that extremely complicated matter, there is one very simple but perhaps very significant fact which may be pointed out. A great many writers today would very definitely reject the thesis propounded by Georg Brandes which Ibsen accepted as a sort of first liberating principle. Brandes, you will remember, stressed the fundamental newness of what he believed to be the spirit of modern literature. Its aims and its standards were proclaimed by him to be essentially different from those of the past, and it was to be tested by different criteria. It is, however, precisely this thesis which Eliot begins by denying and which his disciples at first, second, and third hand tend to follow him in denying.

To them literary excellence is always the same thing. The stress upon tradition means just that. It means that novelty is always superficial, not essential, novelty; it means that for literature there is no such thing as new standards or values. In literature, at least, the great task then becomes not "a war

to the knife" between eras or the crossing of a chasm between the past and the future, but the recovery of a lost
way, a getting back upon the true road, a recapture of that
understanding of the past and of its literature which the
nineteenth century lost. Eliot's *The Waste Land* and Joyce's
Ulysses may seem to the innocent reader to represent des-
perate novelty. But to their admirers they are classic in spirit
—according, of course, to their understanding of what the
classic spirit really is. And I wish merely to suggest the possibility that if Brandes' thesis concerning the valid principles of literary criticism proved so curiously decisive for the
whole course to be taken by Ibsen and those influenced by
him it may possibly be someday apparent that the rejection
of that thesis and the return to a belief that the spirit of all
good literature is essentially the same was equally important.

If that should turn out to be true, then fifty years hence
someone with an ax to grind may undertake to trace how
the literature of the second half of the twentieth century
reveals the steps by which the destruction or transforma-
tion of civilization and human nature was avoided, how the
chasm between the past and the future was revealed to be
an illusion, and why, therefore, the year two thousand found
men living in a world less radically different from that of
nineteen-fifty than such prophets as Shaw had predicted.

I cannot anticipate what the hypothetical polemicists will
say. The most that I can do at this time is to consider the
rather restricted question whether any esteemed playwrights,
especially any of the more recent ones, seem to suggest a re-
versal of direction.

I should, of course, never have given the suggestion that
even in their heyday the modernists seemed to have it all
their own way. In the England of the nineties, for instance,

Sir James Barrie and Bernard Shaw were rivals for popular attention, and Barrie was confessedly old-fashioned in stressing, as he did, the gentler, traditional virtues—persistently implying, for example, that even the New Woman did not exist and that she, like all the supposedly new men, new ideas, and new morals, was a delusion. For a time, moreover, Barrie drew the audiences that Shaw did not. But in the long run he lost out. His plays are seldom revived today, while Shaw's now frequently enjoy longer runs in revivals than they did when they were first produced. Hence if Barrie is evidence of anything, he is evidence on the side of the modernist. It is said that when John Ruskin was asked to write an article attacking the scandalous poetry of Swinburne he replied: "I am righter than he is; but I am no match for him." And even those, if there are any, who think that Barrie was righter than Shaw will have to add the same qualification. Barrie's nostalgic sentiment was no match for Shaw's dynamic and passionate conviction.

A more interesting case was that of the Abbey Theatre of Dublin which had among its avowed purposes resistance to naturalism and to the dominance of Ibsen. This theater became one of the three or four most important theatrical institutions of western Europe. Still existing after more than half a century, it was directly responsible for the production of at least two major playwrights, John Millington Synge and Sean O'Casey. Yet, as the juxtaposition of these two names will suggest, there is at least an open question whether the Abbey Theatre successfully resisted the dominant version of modernism or whether it succumbed to and then abetted it. Let us examine the question.

The Irish National Theatre, as it was first called, was founded by Lady Gregory and William Butler Yeats, two leaders of the Irish Renaissance. Having themselves tried unsuccessfully to write the kind of plays they had in mind, they undertook a systematic and somewhat comic search for wandering Irishmen of talent whom they might convert to the new cause and bring back home to Ireland. Not all their efforts turned out well, as in the case of George Moore, who joined them for a time and then in *Hail and Farewell* wrote three satiric volumes ridiculing the enterprise.

In at least one instance they made a real find in the person of John Millington Synge, a somewhat shadowy young man who had once studied music in Germany but who was, at the moment, living obscurely in Paris supposedly preparing himself to become an English interpreter of French literature. Before long he allowed himself to be convinced of the two fundamental premises of Yeats and Lady Gregory which were, first, that literature is essentially national with its roots in a folk culture and, second, that every writer should put his roots down in his own country and draw his strength from the spirit of his race. Synge abandoned French literature to its fate and went to live in the Aran Islands, whose primitive inhabitants should have remained truly Irish if anybody had.

Out of this somewhat fantastic-sounding adventure came at least two dramatic masterpieces, of which more in a moment. In addition to the plays which Synge wrote, there came also a brief, pointed declaration of the antimodernist principles which Synge, Yeats, and Lady Gregory had evolved. The modern drama and all other forms of modern literature, said Synge, had ceased to be great or even true literature because modern literature had ceased to be at once True and Beautiful. Indeed, to most writers Beauty and Truth presented themselves as irreconcilables, between which a choice must be made. If you chose Beauty, you became an aesthete writing elaborately artificial works which were supposed to be beautiful but were admittedly not true. If, on the other hand, you declared your allegiance to Truth, you became a Naturalist and admitted that the supposed truth which you presented was ugly. But Homer and Shakespeare made no choice. Their works, like all true works of literature, are somehow both True and Beautiful.

This modern impasse, so Synge said, was the inevitable consequence of destroying the folk roots of literature. It was the condition into which the writer could not escape being led if he assumed, as most modern writers did, that literature was based upon and addressed to the members of an intellectual elite rather than to a national folk. The successful artist must return to his own country, and that involved something more than a matter of geographical location. To return to one's own country meant to return to the spirit and the imagination of the simple people of one's race and to draw from that spirit and that imagination both one's theme and one's language. It meant works which would appeal to, as well as be inspired by, the folk. That, in turn, meant the abandonment of such abstract social, moral, and philosophical questions as were concerning the modern drama of Europe in favor of the two things which are really interesting and understandable to a whole folk—namely, the incidents of its own daily life on the one hand, its folk tales and legends on the other. An Irish peasant could not be expected to be interested in either *Ghosts* or *Back to Methuselah*. But he would be interested either in a story of village life or in the story of "Deirdre of the Sorrows."

Moreover, the return to the folk means at least one thing

more. It means the return to a language based upon the speech of the people. The aesthetes wrote a supposedly beautiful language which was dry and dead because it was a purely artificial creation. The Ibsens and the Shaws wrote a language which might be precise and witty but which was also dry and dead because it was the language of the international intellectual and therefore inevitably without flavor. Shakespeare writes a language which is both beautiful (which means poetic) and true (in the sense that it suggests real speech) because it is an improved and polished version of an actual speech. Synge proposed to do with the speech of the inhabitants of the Aran Islands something like what Shakespeare had done with the speech of the Elizabethan Englishman.

Whatever one may think of the theory as theory, there is no doubt about the fact that Synge himself did write plays at least one of which seems like a triumphant justification of the theory. *The Playboy of the Western World* is a delightful comedy as different as one can imagine from anything by Ibsen or Shaw. It is a unique masterpiece, and it does seem in accord with the abstract principles we have been discussing. The language sings an enchanting tune. Though technically prose, it has the flavor of poetry. It is beautiful and at the same time it is true in the sense that it is convincingly founded upon an actual colloquial speech. The subject of the play is the daily life of the people whom it represents and yet it is also at the same time a fable, with its conflict between the father and the son, suggesting one of the recurrent themes of the folk tale. Finally, it probably is true that it is capable of appealing both to the Irish peasant himself and to the members of the international intelligentsia.

Obviously this play, in both theory and practice, is a chal-

lenge to what we have called modernism in the drama—
not a challenge direct by the opposition of idea to idea, but a
challenge in the sense that it simply turns away from "modern ideas" and assumes that such modern ideas are not the
business of literature at all, since its true business is to be
True and Beautiful, not instructive, or analytical, or propa-
gandistic. By no means all Irishmen approved of *The Playboy*. Not all critics have been willing to accept it at its face
value. There have, indeed, been some who have maintained
that Synge, who died early and who held himself personally
rather aloof, was not himself fundamentally sincere and that
he was more of an aesthete "experiencing" simplicity than
genuinely sympathetic with it. Those debates do not, however, really concern us. What does concern us is that the
Abbey Theatre was founded as an antimodernist movement
and that in Synge it found a playwright who successfully
detached himself from what was called "the modern drama."
If he had founded a successful school which followed him,
then the Abbey might be set down as the center of an influence resisting the dominant influence of Ibsen, Shaw, and
the rest.

Many individual geniuses as well as a group program
would have been required to achieve anything of the kind,
and after the premature death of Synge it was a long time
before another outstanding talent appeared. The Abbey
continued to encourage new native playwrights and to produce them. Over a period of twenty years, at least a half
dozen achieved more or less success with plays of Irish life,
often rather sentimental in mood. Then in 1924, almost exactly a generation after Synge, Sean O'Casey's *Juno and the
Paycock* enjoyed what Yeats called ironically "an Irish success"—which means that, like *The Playboy*, it provoked

a riot at its first performance. The Abbey had discovered another major writer.

In everything except essentials *Juno and the Paycock* fitted the program. It dealt with contemporary Irish life; it was thoroughly national in its point of view; the speech of its characters was again a heightened version of the actual colloquial speech of a people. But it was far from being, like *The Playboy*, bubbling and sunny. Somehow the Irish Renaissance had—like so many things in the modern world —gone sour.

What makes the contrast especially striking is the fact that Synge and O'Casey agreed in finding a love of tall talk to be a dominant characteristic of the Irish people. In *The Playboy* this is the thing which makes them poets and tellers of tales. It is also the thing which makes possible the comedy, because only a people absolutely determined to live in a world of wonder could make a hero out of the dismal young man who is the central character of that play. In O'Casey also the characters are great talkers, both about their own exploits and about the glories of Ireland. But they are not poets. They are frauds and blatherskites and liars. Tall talk is an excuse for indolence and cowardice. They murder, they betray, they get drunk. In *The Plough and the Stars*, O'Casey's other most important play, a weak young man chats in the public house with a prostitute while, through the window, drifts the big talk of a patriotic "orator." In *Juno and the Paycock* Captain Boyle—Captain because he had once made a voyage on a coal barge—represents the last stage in the degeneracy of the Irish character corrupted by poetry. In the final scene he staggers into the slum flat of his family from which all the furniture has just been removed by the agents of the installment company. He is ac-

companied by his parasite Joxer—obviously no Irishman is
so poor or so irresponsible as not to support a parasite poorer
and more irresponsible than he—and he is too drunk even
to realize what has happened, too drunk for anything except big talk. Everything, he concludes finally, is in a state
of "chassis," which is, of course, his way of pronouncing
"chaos."

Like the play as a whole, this concluding scene is funny
at the same time that it is bitter, hopeless, and terrible.
It would, in fact, be difficult to find anywhere else in dramatic literature so extraordinary a combination of farce
with loathing and a bleak despair. As I have just pointed out,
the shocking blather of O'Casey's characters is Synge's "Irish
poetry" gone rancid. I might add that many of his characters
are also recognizable versions of the "comic Irishman" familiar in a hundred plays. But instead of playing their part
in sentimental melodrama, they find themselves protagonists
in naturalistic tragedies which might have been inspired by
Zola.

O'Casey makes no effort to harmonize these elements.
The most striking, indeed the almost unique, characteristic
of his plays is the fact that they are one long, unresolved
dissonance. He offers no solution; he proposes no remedy;
he suggests no hope. Artistically as well as intellectually there
is only the clash between the preposterous and the terrible.
Like Captain Boyle, he finds nothing to say except that
"everything is in a state of chassis."

One night, I suppose, offer several partial explanations of
the fact that Synge and O'Casey could give such different
versions of Irish life and character. Synge was dealing with
peasants, O'Casey with members of an urban proletariat.
While poverty in a cottage can be, or at least can be made to

seem, picturesque, poverty in a slum tenement cannot. More-over, the whole personal experience of the two men had been different. Synge was an upper-middle-class intellectual, a good European before he became an Irishman, whereas O'Casey was born into the very poverty and squalor which he described. His formal education was confined to a few weeks in a Catholic school, and from boyhood he worked at hard trades, nursing a fierce resentment and scraping together a few shillings to buy the books from which he educated him-self. Equally important, no doubt, is the fact that between *The Playboy* and *The Plough and the Stars* comes the whole of the Irish Civil War.

Perhaps all these partial explanations can be included within a more general one, which is simply the statement that the whole pull of modern drama and modern literature was in a direction opposite to that taken by Synge and that the pull proved irresistible. It has been in the direction of realism, of sociological concern, of dissonant sonorities, of an obsession with irreconcilable conflicts, and, therefore, in the direction of despair. Even though the Abbey Theatre was founded to resist the pull, one generation was sufficient to make it "modern" in a sense in which it had never wanted to be.

In the plays which we have discussed, neither Synge nor O'Casey reveal an interest in or influence from those philoso-phers of modernism on whom we have laid so much stress. If either had ever read Nietzsche or Freud, for instance, neither appears to have learned anything from them; if O'Casey, long after he had written his best plays, underwent a sort of religious conversion as the result of which he enthusiasti-cally embraced Russian communism as a way out, that conversion was too late to be even retrospectively very significant in connection with either *The Plough and the Stars* or *Juno and the Paycock*. In other words, what was defeated when O'Casey succeeded Synge as the most significant Irish playwright was a literary or aesthetic rather than an ideological protest against modernism. Thinking in exclusively aesthetic terms, Synge had said that great literature must be both True and Beautiful, and he had proposed a subject matter as well as a method for creating such a literature. Though he never put it in these terms, O'Casey admitted that he too found himself compelled to make the choice which so many modernists had implied must be made. He could write beautifully *or* he could write truthfully. He chose to tell what he believed to be the truth, and the truth was, as we moderns have so often found it, ugly.

In my last essay I shall consider more recent, mostly contemporary playwrights, for the purpose of considering whether any of them seem to be moving in any new direction, whether or not the conviction and assumptions of any may fairly be said to indicate an attempt to escape from the dilemmas of modernism.

There are several reasons why the choice of figures which I shall make is bound to seem to some random and why I shall be compelled to speak tentatively. The most obvious of these reasons is simply that a contemporary scene always appears confused and that clear outlines seldom become apparent until the present has become the past. No one can doubt now that Ibsen and Shaw were the dominant figures in their day. Yet during that day many did doubt it. As late as the early twentieth century, William Winter, the most respected American drama critic, was continuing his campaign against Ibsen as an untalented as well as an evil writer and assuring New Yorkers that there was, for example, more genuine drama in Wills's *Olivia* than in the entire corpus of Ibsen's work. But I doubt if very many readers of this book have ever even heard of Wills's *Olivia*. A little later another well-known American critic was editing the collected plays of Henry Arthur Jones and saying in the preface that Jones was demonstrably a far more important writer than Bernard Shaw because he met the most important test—he drew audiences into the theater while Shaw kept them out. Yet even if one grants the validity of the test, it so happened, unfortunately for this critic, that he wrote at just about the moment when Shaw was beginning to fill theaters with the people who were staying away in droves from the plays by Henry Arthur Jones.

It is possible, therefore, that such playwrights as O'Neill, Anderson, Saroyan, Tennessee Williams, and Arthur Miller —to mention only Americans—who seem to many the most interesting the present generation has produced will be as forgotten as Wills a generation hence, while someone whose name does not occur to me is generally admired as the dramatic genius of the mid-twentieth century.

Naturally, this does not seem to me very likely. I feel as sure as one can feel in such matters that those whom I have mentioned are among the best we have produced. Just how good they are is another question. I confess that I doubt strongly that any of them will ever exercise the influence exercised by a Shaw or an Ibsen. What I shall have to say about them would be of more consequence if we thought that they would. But we cannot change the fact. And fortunately it does not render wholly without significance the questions I intend to ask. All of them have attracted audiences, all have been more or less seriously discussed. Are they merely saying at second or third hand what their predecessors had already said? Or do they represent more or less tentative yet recognizable attempts to formulate other premises and reach other conclusions?

6 / How Modern Is the Modern American Drama?

As LONG ago as the late nineteen-twenties I had a conversation with Monsieur Gémier, then director of the Odéon Theater in Paris. I was returning by way of France from a brief inspection of the Russian theater, which was attracting considerable attention at the moment, and I have always remembered Monsieur Gémier's casual remark, "Well, you are coming from Moscow and going to New York—the only two cities in the world where the stage is really interesting today."

At the moment there were probably many people who would have agreed with him. Neither in England, nor France, nor Italy, nor Germany, nor Scandinavia, was there any generation of playwrights who gave promise of taking the place of the pre–World War I generation. In Russia, on the other hand, there were feverish activity and vast enthusiasm for various experiments—many of them extremely eccentric. In America more new plays were being produced per year than had ever been produced in any city of the world before, and for the first time a group of playwrights were taking themselves and dramatic literature with a fundamental seriousness previously unknown in this country.

Moreover, and also for the first time, American plays were being produced in great numbers by the commercial and, sometimes, by the art theaters in Europe. On the one hand, a play by O'Neill had recently become the first American play ever to be offered by one of the state theaters in Paris. On the other, Broadway successes were finding their way to the Broadways of various capitals. I remember, for instance, that I had only a few weeks before seen for the first time *Abie's Irish Rose*, which I had managed to miss in New York but which had caught up with me in, of all places, Budapest. I understood no Hungarian, but it was evident that the audience thought the play very funny.

Almost exactly a quarter of a century has passed since my conversation with Monsieur Gémier, and I doubt that many people today, if they said what he said, would mean quite what he meant. So far as the Russian theater is concerned, very little is heard of it today outside the Russian-dominated countries. Orthodoxy, voluntary or imposed, seems to have frozen its blood. The few recent Russian plays which I have read in translation are little more than prosy and pedestrian embodiments of current propaganda. They are seldom, if ever, produced outside the sphere of Russian political influence, and they have about the same relation to dramatic literature as the moral tales for Sunday-school scholars written by Hannah More in the eighteenth century have to serious fiction.

New York is still one of the most active theatrical capitals, but the hopes which many had in the twenties have not been realized. Every few years since the beginning of the thirties some new playwright has made a successful bid for serious attention. Odets, Saroyan, Tennessee Williams, and Arthur Miller appeared one after another at conveniently spaced intervals. By absolute standards they are as good as, or perhaps better than, all except one—namely, O'Neill—of the playwrights who enlivened the twenties. But they are not as much better than their immediate predecessors as these immediate predecessors were better than any Americans who had preceded them. In the twenties the American drama had started an upward climb which seemed as though it might lead anywhere. There is no longer the feeling that a year hence or two years hence the really great American dramatist may appear and surprise none. Even the staunchest admirers of any one of the men whom I have mentioned would be unlikely to maintain that his work has an impact comparable to that of any one of several European writers of an earlier generation. We have no one who has assumed a stature comparable to that of Shaw or Ibsen no matter by what standards you measure it. Several are worthy of serious consideration; several may be as good as any playwright writing today in any language. But no American of any time has been a really major figure in either the intellectual or the literary world. Four or five Europeans of the late nineteenth and early twentieth centuries were both.

I say this not in order to suggest that our contemporaries are not worth talking about but because I intend to talk about them and simply want to make it clear that, though I take them seriously, neither chauvinism nor anything else prevents me from being aware of the fact that they are not the peers of some of the writers with whom, up to now, we have been concerned. Nevertheless, I want to discuss them not merely because they are the best that we or perhaps anyone else has at the moment, but more especially because I think that they do reveal the fact that in the current drama, and therefore presumably in current thought and feeling, there are trends which suggest an attempt to escape from the dilemma and despair of what I have been calling "modernism."

The very fact that "the modern drama" started late in our country gave it a certain advantage. Just before America entered the First World War the first plays of Eugene O'Neill were produced, and both the Provincetown Players and the Washington Square Players got their start. This, as I have already said, is rather late. By that time Ibsen had been dead for a decade and had been generally recognized for a quarter of a century as the father of the modern drama. By that time Shaw had written most of his important plays, as had the majority of the other European playwrights who achieved world recognition. It seemed almost as though the modern drama in America might take up where the modern drama of Europe had left off.

Moreover, there was a technical reason why this might prove to be an advantage, at least so far as concerns what might be called playwriting as an art as distinguished from playwriting as a method of changing the intellectual atmosphere. After all, classic drama and revolutionary drama are two different things. The plays of Sophocles, of Shakespeare, and of Molière have a certain intellectual content, but they do not, like the plays of Ibsen, make any attempt radically to alter the intellectual concepts of the audience for which they were written. A recognition of this fact is the real meaning behind Shaw's gibe that Shakespeare was a man whose ideas were the ideas of the Elizabethan man in the street. Shakespeare, added Shaw, "borrowed his morality; I invented mine." And there is a very important sense in which that is true. Shakespeare is a classic dramatist not only in the sense that he is a great and important one but in the sense that he was not a revolutionary dramatist.

By 1916 even in the United States intellectuals were familiar with the radical ideas of the European modern drama and in a general way accepted them. What had once been "advanced thought" was just on the point of becoming the ideas of the man in the street. So true was this that many once exciting passages in Ibsen's plays were already beginning to seem, as they do today, almost fatuous, because the point of view for which they are arguing is taken for granted. Thus the debate at the end of A Doll's House, with Nora's solemn insistence upon her right to be true to herself rather than to the outworn conventions of nineteenth-century domesticity, sounds almost like a parody on the serious female thinker. In similar fashion when, in Ghosts, Mrs. Alving makes a plea for books which face the truth, she seems at best to be overlaboring an argument which was won long ago.

What this means is that by 1916 the American dramatist might have undertaken to write "classical plays" in the sense that, instead of arguing the theses of modernism, he might have taken them for granted or, to put it another way, assumed that the "revolutionary" had become "classic." To a certain extent that is precisely what he did do in a way which I shall illustrate by citing two extremely popular plays, both of which happened to have been produced in the fall of 1924 and one of which has since been revived, not too successfully.

In *What Price Glory* Laurence Stallings and Maxwell Anderson wrote a melodramatic farce about war which took it for granted that the audience was ready to think about soldiers, not in terms of any *dulce et decorum est . . . ,* but in terms of a "modern" disillusion with the whole concept of military glory. In *They Knew What They Wanted* Sidney Howard introduced the mother of an illegitimate child over whom so many modern dramatists had argued, but Howard simply took it for granted that his audience would require no argument to believe her pardonable and would assume, as a matter of course, that his heroine was guilty of no serious dereliction. Stallings and Anderson as well as Howard were really "borrowing their morality." In a sense not true of Ibsen or Shaw their ideas were, to return to Shaw's phrase, "the ideas of the man in the street." True, the man in the street had not had these ideas very long. Moreover, he had them now only because of a revolution in which Ibsen and Shaw had played important roles. But he did have them; or at least he was willing to accept them when they were assumed in a play—as the first audiences of his predecessors had not been. That, of course, is one of the reasons why Shaw and Ibsen had to build an audience slowly, while Stallings, Anderson, and Howard woke up next morning to find themselves famous.

It may have occurred to some of you that there is an apparent inconsistency in some of the things which I have just been saying. On the one hand, I have suggested that the new American playwrights were less concerned with "new ideas" or, indeed, with any abstract ideas as such than their

European predecessors. On the other hand, I began my discussion by suggesting that in the Americans we might find signs of certain attitudes which suggested the beginnings of a perhaps unconscious protest against the bleakness of fully developed "modernism."

I have said both of these things, but they are not actually incompatible however much they may seem at first sight to be so. The reasons why they are not are somewhat elusive, but I shall try to be as explicit about them as possible.

Suppose we begin by saying that the effect of a body of literature, especially the effect of what we call classical literature, does not depend exclusively upon the argument which it presents or even upon ideas which are explicitly expounded. If it did, then the importance of literature, or at least of any except didactic literature, to society would be as slight as unimaginative people often assume that it is. To them novels, poems, and plays are merely rather vague and dubiously logical ways of saying what could be said much more effectively in other ways. But even the social importance of great literature is immeasurable just because it communicates attitudes which cannot be communicated in any other way. When Hamlet exclaims, "What a creature is man," he is making an exclamatory statement. But the effect of the play upon the audience's whole feeling about the creature man depends less upon this statement than upon the fact that the play as a whole treats and presents man as a being in connection with whom that exclamation becomes obviously appropriate.

Even when literal-minded people are brought to admit this, they are likely to continue to feel that it represents a danger. The poet takes unfair advantage of "emotionalism." He convinces people of things which are not true. He trades on the semantic errors rife in any emotional presentation. We would all, the literal minded think, be much better off if nothing was ever stated except in logical terms and without the use of any words not to be found in basic English.

On the other hand, those of us who think of literature, not as merely a collection of vain if sometimes pleasant fancies, but as one of the ways of knowing and one of the methods of communication would insist that it discovers and communicates actual truths about human experience of which logical analysis leaves us completely ignorant— that *Hamlet* tells us something about the human spirit which no philosophical or psychological treatise ever did or could tell us and that these things are as true as any of the things which the treatises do present.

We would go even further than that. We would suggest that one of the important reasons why "modernism" ended by seeming so bleak and dispirited is simply that modernist writers failed to recognize the fact that the poetic and the dramatic are true, that the refusal to accept Sophocles and Shakespeare as part of the evidence helps to make modern life look drab. You cannot say, for instance, that love is nothing but a biological urge or that patriotism is nothing but tribal xenophobia unless you say that *Romeo and Juliet* and the last play in the Agamemnon trilogy do not mean anything. They do mean something. They mean that men and women can "love," not merely submit to biological urges, that they can revere the idea of justice, not merely stand up for the mores of their tribe. The strangest thing of all is that in so far as many moderns grant this at all they grant it only in connection with those imaginative presentations which are pessimistic or disillusioning. To them Molly Bloom's soliloquy at the end of *Ulysses* means something;

Hamlet's soliloquy or Romeo's soliloquy does not. One is truth; the other is fiction.

The bearing of all this on what I said earlier when I was accusing myself of an apparent inconsistency is, I hope, clear. To turn away from argument, to write drama which shows some tendency to accept rather than to argue for any given set of ideas, is inevitably, if the resulting work has any content at all, to depend for one's effect more and more upon these modes of feeling and thinking as well as those methods of presentation which are exclusively literary. And it is part of my contention that a first step by literature in the direction of what might finally become a salvation was taken when playwrights showed a tendency to be more interested in displaying human life against a certain background of moral assumptions than in presenting the argumentative defense of those assumptions.

By no stretch of the imagination could either *What Price Glory* or *They Knew What They Wanted* be called great plays. Yet even they could be used to demonstrate that because they were not primarily didactic the first was able to say about war and the second was able to say about love certain things which had not recently been said in serious plays. They attempted to concern themselves with the quality of human experience rather than with an analysis of its rational elements. It is when one considers the quality of human experience that human life is most likely to come to seem worthy of respect and of admiration.

One would, I think, be safe enough in making some such guarded statement as the following. During the quarter of a century just past several American playwrights of repute have written plays in which either some moral problem is considered from a point of view involving considerations that seem to come from "the past" rather than from the theoretical "future" of the modernists or, if no moral problem is specifically posed, then what I have called the quality of human experience, rather than some devitalizing analysis of it, is presented as the crucial test of the value and meaningfulness of human life. I shall not risk any evaluation of these plays. I shall not contend that they are of outstanding excellence when judged by absolute standards. Neither can I give any assurance that the trend which they seem to me to reveal actually means that they are effectively proclaiming the future course of literary expression in the drama or elsewhere. They may represent only survivals or weak protests. But at least the phenomenon can be observed, and some comment must be made upon it to round out the whole discussion upon which we embarked.

Instead of considering these dramatists one by one as individuals, I suggest that we might instead consider two characteristics of the sort I have been trying to suggest and then see what examples may be cited to prove that these characteristics really have been exhibited by recent American playwrights. Let us ask such questions as the following. Have any of these playwrights tended to make the dramatic form rather than any specific political, social, or even moral thesis the means of conveying their meaning? Have they announced theses which imply some return to the past?

My first question concerning the recognition of a literary form as itself highly significant is a very crucial one, and few things were more characteristic of the modern drama than its indifference to the rules supposed to govern the forms. On the one hand Shaw, though he would to be sure have called himself a comic writer, habitually chooses farcical plots and farcical dialogue to treat his most serious themes, as he does in *Androcles and the Lion*, which is concerned with the residual realities which he finds in Christianity, and in *Back to Methuselah*, which is concerned with the ultimate destiny of mankind. Ibsen would hardly have been troubled by an attempt to demonstrate that *Ghosts* violated even the more fundamental of the "rules of Aristotle," and though *The Wild Duck* ends with a peculiarly distressing death, he himself spoke of the play in a letter as "a bit of tomfoolery," as though he thought of it as sort of farce—which in one aspect it is. Neither he nor Shaw was in the slightest degree concerned with what would once have been called "propriety."

The critic-defenders of the modern drama were even more concerned than the dramatists themselves with the revolt against the forms as well as the themes of the past. It was said, for example, that one important distinction between such a modern tragedy as *Ghosts* and almost any traditional tragedy is that whereas the older tragedy comes to an end the modern tragedy goes on. Thus Hamlet dies, and with the entry of Fortinbras the story comes to an end. Mrs. Alving, on the other hand, lives to face indefinitely the unsolved problem. Evil, in other words, is not self-limiting as in the older conception, but endless. Others insisted that an even more fundamental difference lay in the nature of the tragic hero. Classical tragedy was aristocratic, was based upon acceptance of the idea of the great or at least the superior man. Modern tragedy was, on the contrary, democratic and concerned with the usual or average man, so that Gerhart Hauptmann's play *The Weavers* was held up for especial admiration because its protagonist was said to be not an individual but a class—the mass or the proletariat. Presently, and to go even further, it was being said that the fundamental error of all previous conceptions of the nature of tragedy lay in its avowed intention to "purge the soul." Such an intention, it was added, could only be voiced in a society devoted to maintaining a status quo. To purge the soul, to relieve it of its stress, is to promote an acquiescence in things as they are. The modern drama, on the contrary, is revolutionary in its purpose. It does not want to purge the soul but to burden it to the point where it will rebel against things as they are. When one has witnessed a performance of *Hamlet*, one does not want to do anything, but when one has seen *The Weavers*, one wants to mount the barricades. From this argument it is obviously but a step to what soon became Marxist's formulation: "Art is a Weapon."

Sometimes the revolt against traditional forms seems to have been based largely upon the feeling that "form," being merely external and artificial, makes no positive contribution to the total effect of the work, and to those who felt thus the important thing was simply that formal considerations should not be permitted to interfere with the playwright's expression. At other times the demand for new forms was accompanied by the realization that new forms contribute to the effect of new ideas, and the followers and the elaborators of Strindberg's dream techniques were aware of this fact. If you are going to say that life is meaningless, you cannot effectively say it in a play where the play itself constitutes meaning; the violence and confusion of the play must express the violence and confusion which it proclaims. If life is a nightmare, then dramas must be nightmarish. It is impossible to deny that life is significant if the form which you impose upon a representation of it tends to give it meaning.

To put the whole thing in another way, one might say that

the abandonment or destruction of the Tragic Form is logically connected with all the other things which modernism in the drama abandoned or destroyed. It is a consequence of the general tendencies, because conventional tragedy rests upon assumptions concerning the reality of the ego, the supreme importance of man in a universe where he is only a little below the angels, and the responsibility of the individual for his own conduct. Moreover, if what I have been trying to say is true, it is more than merely a consequence; it is also a cause. Plays in the conventional tragic form are one of the means by which man's confidence in his own importance and responsibility is expressed and communicated. Without believing certain things about man you cannot, on the one hand, write tragedies. Without tragedies one is, on the other hand, not nearly so likely to believe those same things. Literature is not merely a description of the human environment. To remove tragedy from it is to remove the possibility of one kind of ennobling experience. Tragedy asserts the dignity of man. But unless what I have been saying is false, tragedy is also an evidence of that same dignity. If all this seems elusive, perhaps I can explain it by an analogy.

Everybody knows La Rochefoucauld's famous remark that if it were not for poetry very few people would ever fall in love. No doubt this is true and may be truly taken to mean that love and literature are closely related inventions. But it is false to assume, as most admirers of La Rochefoucauld do, that to admit this is the equivalent of admitting that what we call love "really is" only a biological urge dressed up in the insubstantial fictions of a poet. Poetic experience is a fact as undeniably real as any biological urge. If few would love were it not for poetry, it is equally true that if men had not been able to love no one would ever have written poetry. That poetry exists is proof of the existence of love. Similarly, that tragedy exists is proof that man is a creature capable of dignity and significance.

Under the circumstances is it not significant that two of the best-known and most ambitious American playwrights of our day, Eugene O'Neill and Maxwell Anderson, could be most simply classified as writers of tragedy? In the case of no earlier modern whom I have mentioned would a reference to the form preferred be an obvious element in a compact description. Neither Ibsen, nor Strindberg, nor Shaw, nor Chekhov, nor Pirandello are thought of first as writers of tragedy or of comedy. The defining terms of which one first thinks are sociological, or psychological, or political, or moral, not literary. But O'Neill and Anderson are men whose most serious effort has obviously been to write for moderns plays which have some of the essential characteristics of traditional tragedy. The significance of this fact does not depend entirely on the answer to the question: How good by absolute standards are their tragedies? No matter what answer one gives to that question, the fact remains that both represent a reaction against what I have described as "modernism in the drama" by virtue of the assumption, instinctive in O'Neill's case, more self-conscious in that of Anderson, that their response to the spectacle of human life is one which can best be expressed and communicated in the form most obviously implying faith in, as well as respect for, the human spirit.

In every other aspect the temperaments and the talents of the two men are in marked contrast. O'Neill is by far the more tempestuous of the two. I have previously remarked that he has declared his indebtedness to Strindberg, and this, I must add, makes it almost unnecessary to say that he has always been far from at peace with himself. In him and his writing alike there are strong impulses in the direction of Strindbergian pessimism with Dionysian overtones. In the most recent of his plays performed in New York, *The Iceman Cometh*, he seems to have given way almost completely to nihilism. No spectator who has followed his plays one after another, however, is likely to suppose that such pessimistic views are a constant, or in my opinion the most striking, aspect of his work. In his most notable tragedies, the tension is created by the conflict between Strindbergianism and an opposite determination to confer upon man a tragic dignity.

O'Neill's most persistent theme is what has sometimes been called the theme of "belonging." From the earliest one-act plays of the sea down at least to *Mourning Becomes Electra* his most nearly heroic figures have always been those who, like Yank in *The Hairy Ape* or Ephraim Cabot in *Desire under the Elms*, belong to something larger than themselves which confers dignity and importance upon them. They are not, like Oswald Alving, mean victims. They are men of heroic stature determined to find in the universe something besides themselves to which they can belong and be loyal. They are, in other words, tragic heroes.

"Behind the smaller themes of all my plays," so O'Neill once wrote, "lies a larger theme, namely, that sickness of today which is caused by man's loss of religion and his need to find some substitute for it." Or, as in conversation he once remarked: "I am not interested in plays which are merely about the relation of man to man. I am interested in nothing except the relation of man to God."

One may say, and be right in saying, that by "God"

O'Neill means whatever in the universe may be outside of and larger than man's self. But the fact remains that the search for or the finding of that thing outside himself to which man belongs is the theme of all traditional tragedy. O'Neill is "not interested," I repeat, in plays about the relation of man to man. But what is more characteristic of what I have been calling "modernism" than the denial that there is any subject except the relation of man to man, that there is anything except other men with which man can have any significant relation?

Maxwell Anderson's temperament is a far less tempestuous one, and it is characteristic of the difference between the two men that they should have approached by different routes their discovery that tragedy was, for each, his central concern. O'Neill began with Strindberg, found himself as member of a radical bohemian group superficially interested in various politico-social questions, and only gradually came to realize that what he was really seeking and what he hoped in *Mourning Becomes Electra* he had found was something closely equivalent to Greek tragedy. Anderson, on the other hand, began as a writer for the popular theater, and when in the verse play *Elizabeth the Queen* he first revealed his ambition to write tragedy, he adopted a method almost academically conventional and imitated the most superficial aspects of traditional tragedy by employing a familiar historical subject and by writing in romantic verse. Not only *Elizabeth the Queen* but the whole series of romantic plays which followed it, including *Mary of Scotland* and *The Masque of Kings* as well as several other less successful plays, were far more Victorian than either Greek or Elizabethan, rather more in the tradition of Tennyson or the American George Henry Boker than in that of Sophocles or Shake-

speare. To put it another way, O'Neill found his subject
before he realized that it was a traditional, tragic subject;
Anderson wrote highly traditional or perhaps merely conventional tragedies before he discovered his subject. Nevertheless Anderson also did discover that subject, and in at
least two plays, most notably in *Winterset*, he gave an expression which no doubt falls short of greatness but which
is quite adequate to define the subject.

That subject turns out to be one which may ultimately be
the same as O'Neill's but which is, nevertheless, plainly a
different aspect of it. O'Neill's theme, as I have tried to say,
is man's achievement of significant stature through the estab-
lishment of a relation with something outside himself and
outside of man. Anderson's theme is more specifically moral.
In *Winterset* as well as in the less successful *Key Largo*, the
fable involves the fate of persons who have lost their capacity to believe in right and wrong as absolutes but who
find, nevertheless, that without this belief a successful life
is impossible. If O'Neill insists upon the indispensability
or some sort of religion, Anderson insists in his turn upon
the equal indispensability of ethical standards.

In *Winterset*, the action takes place some twenty years
after a certain radical agitator has been executed for a crime
he did not commit. His was a *cause célèbre* and cannot be
forgot. Recently new evidence has come to light, and there
is a possibility that the truth will be revealed at last. To a
whole group of people that will make, even twenty years
later, a vast difference. The criminal who was actually guilty,
an acquaintance who saw the crime committed, the son of
the martyred man, and the judge who presided over the
trial which went wrong are all drawn, in one way or another,

together again, each hoping or fearing that the truth will at last be known.

Obviously the initial situation suggests the Sacco-Vanzetti case. As a matter of fact Maxwell Anderson had, a few years before, written in collaboration with another playwright a topical play based directly upon the story of that case. It is plain that Anderson saw in it the material for a tragedy also, and it is interesting to see what must happen if the story is to be treated, not as journalistic comment, but as tragedy. For one thing, the action is placed twenty years later in order to reveal the fact that the consequences are not merely local but continue to be felt as long as the wrong continues to echo in men's minds and lives. More importantly, the theme must become, not mere social criticism, but a consideration of the meaning and importance of Justice.

All the characters in the play are in one way or another "modern"; this means that no one is sure that he knows what Justice is, that it exists outside his own mind, that it is more than the mores of his group, or that any sensible man would sacrifice any real advantage in the interest of such an abstraction. Yet, with one exception, all the characters are troubled by their concern with something in which they are not sure that they believe. The dead man's son has devoted his life to the task of rehabilitating his father's reputation. The unjust judge, grown old and half insane, wanders about the city explaining to strangers why he did what he thought was best. The man who knows what really happened waits in fear and self-loathing because he has never had the courage to tell the truth.

Thus, so the play seems to say, though justice cannot be defined neither can it be dismissed. Here is a group of men who have lost all simple unquestioning allegiance to a traditional code and whose purely rational minds have been unable to supply them with reasons why they should do anything except look after their own interests. Yet they are men, and as men they cannot help loving justice. The only person in the play untroubled by such considerations is the actual murderer. This world of moral anarchy is, for him, the best of all possible worlds. Such a world inevitably is a gangsters' world. Only a gangster functions well in it. Perhaps, one may add, if it lasts long enough all men will be gangsters.

Anderson, as I have already mentioned, returned to a somewhat similar theme in *Key Largo*. I shall not attempt to discuss either it or *Winterset* any further except to say, first, that both seem to me indubitably attempts to write tragedy in a traditional sense and, second, that the special tragic themes which they treat may very well come to seem, of all possible tragic themes, those most relevant to us. O'Neill found the sickness of today to be the result of our loss of all religious conviction. Anderson finds it to be the loss of any ethical standards to which our minds can give assent. But the two things are aspects of the same thing, and they both see man in the same tragic dilemma. Because man is man, he cannot comfortably inhabit a meaningless universe in which even good and evil are merely relative. Because he is a modern man, he has nevertheless trained himself to think in ways which inevitably make him see the universe as meaningless and "right" and "wrong" as merely words.

When Ibsen proclaimed that truths grow old, he did not intend to create an ethical vacuum. As I said when we first began to consider him, he remained to the end a moralist in his own way. But whatever his intentions, it is difficult not to suspect that his ethical relativity has led, logically or illogically and step by step, to a situation impossible for the human being to live with. I rest my case for O'Neill and Anderson as modern American playwrights who are anti-modernists not only upon the fact that both see the traditional form of tragedy as in itself a significant comment on a world which has lost its sense of human dignity but also upon the fact that both chose as the most important theme of their tragedies man's persistent desire to be noble in a sense which one dominant kind of rationalism insists does not really make sense.

It is necessary to bring to an end this discussion of what may someday be seen as a manifestation in the theater of the beginning of a significant revolt against the despair of a Shaw or a Strindberg, the beginning of an attempt to give man again a view of the universe which would make it a fit place for human habitation.

If it were possible, I should like to consider the work of more recently successful playwrights, notably Tennessee Williams and Arthur Miller, and to ask whether they also afford any support to the hope that at least the makers of fiction recognize the need and the desire for some positive confession of faith in that spirit of man which rebels against the attempt to confine him within the limits of a purely mechanical and inhuman universe. I shall have to be content, however, with one or two very brief suggestions.

Neither Miller's *Death of a Salesman* nor Tennessee Williams' *A Streetcar Named Desire* is a cheerful play. Both end with what looks less like a tragic affirmation than like a simple confession of defeat. Neither Willy Loman nor Blanche Dubois is likely to strike the spectator as a very dignified or very noble character, and both are completely destroyed—as, say, Hamlet and Othello are not completely destroyed—when the story ends. Loman is a suicide and Blanche is being led away to a madhouse.

Obviously neither Miller nor Williams plainly commits himself as do Maxwell Anderson and O'Neill to either the form or the ethical content of classic tragedy. Moreover, neither exhibits, as plainly as it seems to me O'Neill exhibits, a determination to seek persistently for something in the universe outside man to which he can appeal and "belong." It is possible to interpret *Death of a Salesman* as brutal naturalism and *A Streetcar Named Desire* as a sort of semi-surrealist version of the Strindbergian submission to destructive obsessions.

If such is a proper summation, then Miller and Williams, the two most widely discussed American playwrights of the moment, follow O'Neill and Anderson only as Sean O'Casey followed Synge. They represent, that is to say, the collapse of a reaction and illustrate, as did O'Casey, an irresistible pull in the direction of nihilism and despair.

Perhaps, indeed, that is the proper interpretation to be put upon their work and their current popularity. I am unwilling, however, to leave the subject without suggesting the possibility that there may be something to be said on the other side, and at the risk of being accused of overinterpretation, I should like to say it.

So far as *Death of a Salesman* is concerned, it seems reasonable to suppose that it is intended as something a little more than merely detached "scientific" naturalism. Most spectators, I think, assume that it embodies some "social criticism," and most, I imagine, assume that the social criticism is of a sort by now very traditional. In this view, Willy

Loman is the victim of an unjust competitive society. He was first corrupted by its false ideals and then exploited by those shrewder and more ruthless than himself. Society made him what he was, and in a better society his fate would have been a happier one. In all this there is, of course, nothing incompatible with what I have been loosely calling "modernism." The doctrine and methods of the naturalists lend themselves very readily to such "social significance."

What makes it impossible to dismiss *Death of a Salesman* as merely left-wing naturalism is the curious fact that Miller himself seems to be some sort of pluralist and that his play could be interpreted, not as a demonstration of the workings of social determinism, but as a study of the effects of moral weakness and irresponsibility. Willy Loman is a victim of society, but he is also a victim of himself. He accepted an essentially vulgar and debased as well as a false system of values. He himself says, and the audience seems to be expected to believe him, that he might have led a happy life if he had followed his own bent and become, for example, a carpenter, instead of submitting to the prejudice which makes a salesman more respectable than a man who works with his hands. His tragic guilt—and it is his, not society's —was, in this view, a very old-fashioned one. He was not true to himself. Thus the moral of the play becomes a classical moral and must necessarily presume both the existence of the classical ego and the power to make a choice.

Seen in this light, Miller becomes a moralist, at least in the sense and in much the same fashion that Ibsen was still a moralist. He has found his way back along the road which leads to determinism and the disappearance of the ego at least to the point where the dramatic disciples of Ibsen first entered upon it, and *Death of a Salesman* thus becomes a qualified reaffirmation of the individual's privilege of being, within certain limits, what he chooses to be.

The case of Tennessee Williams is different but equally dubious. As I have already suggested, the most obvious interpretations put him plainly among the despairing explorers of pathological states of mind just as the obvious interpretations put Arthur Miller among the sociological naturalists. In all his most striking plays, *The Glass Menagerie, Summer and Smoke,* and *A Streetcar Named Desire,* the chief character is obsessed, and in the last two the obsession takes a sexual form. Madness seems to interest the author more than anything else, and at least in the third and most successful of the plays a quasi-expressionist technique is used for the purpose of persuading the audience to see certain of the events from the standpoint of the heroine's abnormality rather than from its own presumably objective point of view.

In each of the three plays there is another recurrent theme. Each of the heroines numbers among her obsessions the fact that she is or was "a lady." In each the ideal of respectability, the sense that her parents and her remoter ancestors lived in accordance with some code to which she herself would like to be loyal but which no one with whom she comes in contact acknowledges, is so strong as to appear crucial. In *The Glass Menagerie* the mother sees her family disintegrating because it no longer finds her dream of respectability anything but annoying. In both *Summer and Smoke* and *A Streetcar Named Desire* the heroine seems to succumb to crude sexuality because she has so fanatically refused to accept a normal life among people who appear to her as hopelessly unrefined.

Tennessee Williams grew up in the South. Like so many

other Southern writers, the existence of a decayed aristocracy was one of the inescapable facts of the society with which he was most familiar. That representatives of such a decayed aristocracy should appear in his plays may mean no more than that they were part of his experience. Nevertheless it seems to me obvious that his persistent concern with them does have a greater significance. These helpless survivors from the past, feeble and pathetic clingers to a dead tradition, take on the importance of symbols. They are not accidental facts; they mean something.

Upon the answer to the question "What do they mean? Of what are they symbols?" depends the whole meaning of the plays so far as our own special theme is concerned. Let us consider it in connection with A Streetcar Named Desire.

Blanche DuBois, a decayed aristocrat and a fanatical lady, has already lost her position as a schoolteacher because she is also a nymphomaniac. As the curtain rises we see her arriving alone and seeking refuge in the squalid home of her sister Stella, who has married a crude and brutal young man of foreign extraction. This sister has made what the psychologists would call "a satisfactory adjustment." She has rejected and forgotten the traditions of her past. She has accepted the frank squalor of her surroundings and the ignorant brutality of her husband, chiefly because she is reveling delightedly in his abundant and animalistic sexuality. Blanche, the nymphomaniac, is horrified by what some would call her sister's "normality." She makes a feeble and ridiculous attempt to instruct both the sister and the husband in the genteel tradition, and she is violently repelled by their contented animality. But because she can neither lead their life nor the genteel life of which she dreams, her last defenses crumble and she is led away to an asylum, certifiably insane.

Everything depends upon, as the phrase goes, which side the author is on. It appears that to many members of the audience this question presents no difficulty. They are, and they assume that the author is, on the side of the sister. She is "healthy," "adjusted," "normal." She lives in the present; she accepts things as they are; and she will never be confined to a madhouse. Her husband is crude, even somewhat brutal, but he is also virile; he is the natural man and one of literature's many kinsmen of Lady Chatterley's lover. Virility, even orgiastic virility, is the proper answer to decadence. Stella, the representative of a decayed aristocracy, is rejuvenated by a union with a representative of "the people."

Even more conspicuously than in the case of Arthur Miller's play, an alternate reading of the situation is possible. In Miller one suspects a sort of pluralism. In Williams the question presents itself instead under the form of an ambiguity.

By this I meant that while one section of the audience takes the side of Stella almost as a matter of course another section understands and shares Blanche's revulsion. Her instincts are right. She is on the side of civilization and refinement. But the age has placed her in a tragic dilemma. She looks about for a tradition according to which she may live and a civilization to which she can be loyal. She finds none. Ours is a society which has lost its shape.

Behind her lies a past which, at least in retrospect, seems to have been civilized. The culture of the Old South is dead, and she has good reason to know that it is. It is, however, the only culture about which she knows anything. The world of Stella and of her husband is a barbarism,—perhaps, as its admirers would say, a vigorous barbarism—but a barbarism nonetheless. Blanche chooses the dead past and becomes the victim of that impossible choice. But she does choose it rather than the "adjustment" of her sister. At least she has not succumbed to barbarism.

As I have said, one's choice of sides will depend largely upon one's attitude toward Stella's "virile" husband. The real question is whether he is villain or hero. If we knew which he is to his creator, we should know whether Williams should be classified among that group of "moderns" who see in a return to the primitive the possible rejuvenation of mankind or whether he belongs rather with traditionalists, such as the esoteric T. S. Eliot on the one hand or the popular Maxwell Anderson on the other, who maintain that from the past itself we shall still have to learn if we are ever to learn at all what civilization means.

I cannot tell you what Williams thinks or says. I can, after due warning, report a very significant thing which he is said to have said. At third hand I have it that when queried in conversation about the meaning of A *Streetcar Named Desire*, or rather about the significance of its chief male character, he replied: "It means that if you do not watch out the apes will take over."

If this report is accurate, and I repeat that I have it only at third hand, the question is answered. Williams, despite all the violence of his plays, despite what sometimes looks very much like nihilism, is really on the side of what modernists would call the Past rather than the Future—which means, of course, on the side of those who believe that the future, if there is to be any civilized future, will be less new than most modern dramatists from Ibsen on have professed to believe.

In fact, the thesis which from the very beginning I have been attempting to expound might be summed in such a way as to include a phrase from Williams' alleged comment. That is, a break with the past as radical as that which much modern thought and much modern drama seems to advocate unintentionally prepares the way for the apes to take over. A civilized man is likely to find it increasingly difficult to live in either the physical or the spiritual world which has gradually been evolving. It offers him neither the physical nor the spiritual peace without which he cannot exist. But the apes, like the gangster in *Winterset*, find it not uncongenial. They can survive the physical chaos, and they are not aware of the spiritual one.

When Ibsen joyfully hailed the appearance of a chasm between the past and the future, he was not aware of all that it implied. Actually and at a minimum, it implied the end of post-Renaissance civilization. Even if the optimists are right and a civilization across the chasm is possible, it will have to be one discontinuous with that which had been evolving from about the thirteenth century almost to the end of the nineteenth. And to those of us who are loyal to the culture into which we were born, even the optimists' predictions are catastrophic.

Perhaps, by way of conclusion, I may be allowed to rephrase a thesis which I recently stated elsewhere. To do this will both avoid simple repetition of what I have been saying at length and at the same time enable me to state a similar proposition in somewhat different terms.

What I have just called post-Renaissance civilization rests upon many premises, among which the following are crucial. First, man is a creature capable of dignity. Second, life as led in this world, not merely life as it might be led either in the Christian's City of God or the Marxist's Socialist

State, is worth living. Third, the realm of human rationality is the realm in which man may most fruitfully live.

An astonishing proportion of all serious modern works of literature imply the rejection of one or more of these premises. When determinism, psychological or economic, has deprived man of even a limited power of self-determination and at the same time denied the validity of any of the ethical beliefs to which he may be attached, then man has ceased to have dignity. When either the radical pessimist or the Utopian reformer has represented life "under the present social system" as inevitably frustrated or defeated, then the Renaissance thesis that life in this world is worth living is denied. When the subject of fiction becomes, as it so often does become, the obsessions, fixations, neuroses, and perversions to which the human psyche sometimes falls victim, then the premise which states that human rationality is the most important human realm is also denied.

During the past three-quarters of a century the drama has been a more significant branch of literature than it was during the two centuries before. The modern drama is, however, open to the same charge that may be made against modern literature as a whole. Its tendency has been to undermine the foundations of post-Renaissance civilization.

/ The Messenger Lectures

IN ITS original form this book consisted of six lectures delivered at Cornell University in October, 1952, namely, the Messenger Lectures on the Evolution of Civilization. That series was founded and its title prescribed by Hiram J. Messenger, B.Litt., Ph.D., of Hartford, Connecticut, who directed in his will that a portion of his estate be given to Cornell University and used to provide annually a "course or courses of lectures on the evolution of civilization, for the special purpose of raising the moral standard of our political, business, and social life." The lectureship was established in 1923.

/ Index

135